ARISE SHINE

Sister in Christ.

You are God's masterpiece!
Ephesian 2:10 :)

Rachel Inouye

Awaken to Your True Identity in Christ

RACHEL INOUYE

Copyright

Dedication

For Michael.

For how you have supported me in everything I've ever toyed with, attempted, or done.

For being a wonderful provider, best friend, husband and my amazing forerunner! Without you, none of this would ever be a THANG!

You've edited and formatted our lives, not just this book. You make me radiant!

I love you always and in all ways.

Rachel

Contents:

Introduction

Arise, shine, for your light has come, and the glory of the LORD has risen upon you. Isaiah 60:1

You are the beloved. You are sealed and secure in Christ, awakening to the truth of who you are and your true identity is a game changer. This truth will help you get off the porch, break out of the box of limitation you've believed about yourself or God and embolden you to leave the pew because you are made to SHINE! The world is waiting and watching.

I am a storyteller. I will be making my points about identity, a subject I'm quite passionate about, mainly through story and Scriptures. So let's get started. When we are able to truly say, "I know who I am! I know whose I am and I honor Who You Are." GAME OVER! Knowing who we are in Christ and awakening to this truth should/will cause a reaction: It's an upgrade. Get off the porch. Break out of the box and leave the pew.

A secure identity in Christ is not only foundational, it's a game changer!

GAME OVER - when we find out who we are in Christ and walk in it... Seriously, game over! Because what follows a secured identity is a world changer. Each life affects the lives around us and yours is influencing someone's all the time.

I am a storyteller and I want to start this book about identity with a tribute to a master storyteller and artist, my father, Richard Heggen. I wrote this for my father and sent it to him years before he died. Even though he has passed and the verb should be used in past tense I'm going to include it here just like it was written when I sent it to him.

Richard Heggen: A Tribute - Something given or done as an expression of esteem.

I'm so grateful to God for many things in my life: my salvation purchased at Christ's expense, His mercy, love and care in my life have been so evident.

It amazes me to think that the God of the universe, the sovereign one over all creation, the one who flung the stars in space and calls each of them by name, the one who tells the seas how far they can go and gives them their borders and boundaries, the one who made every animal and every planet also created me. And when this sovereign God of the universe created me he gave me a mother and father. It was God's design that I would be Richard Heggen's daughter. And for that tremendous blessing, I praise His name.

My dad showed me love in more ways than this short tribute can attest to. He has spent time with me, counseled me, guided me, taught me, laughed with me, shopped with me, eaten with me and we have sung together for years. That is one of my earliest vivid memories of time spent with him.
We would sing "Little White Duck" together for fun or for an audience. He taught me my first three chords on the guitar! I could play a mean "Shoofly Don't Bother Me" thanks to my Dad! We have sung spirituals like "May the Circle Be Unbroken" and hymns like "Amazing Grace," "What a Friend We Have in Jesus" and "He Touched Me," just to name a few.

We have sung Elvis' "Blue Suede Shoes" and Patsy Cline's "Crazy" I have fond memories of my father singing and playing the guitar in the living room while I tried to fall asleep in the bedroom down the hall. I still remember late-night worship sessions held in our small living room. With people crammed in singing to God with both electric and acoustic guitars playing and tambourines jingling… it was never about performing perfectly but always occurred with great worship and sweet fellowship experienced by all. I've often wondered what our neighbors may have thought. Could they even hear? I think sometimes they attended.

I always tried my best to strum my guitar as my dad would fiddle around on the electric guitar or play the booming line of his bass. I sometimes felt frustrated, because I couldn't play by ear like he did or figure out new keys, but my dad never made me feel inferior or squelched my love for playing music with him.

I also remember going places with my dad. I liked to get in our pick-up truck or camper and head to downtown Ames with him. One time we drove all the way down there, parked and then laughed because he couldn't remember why it was we came. It didn't matter! I still had fun! Even running errands together could be an adventure. If we got the car washed, drove to the corner gas station parking lot where a farmer sold sweet corn off his flatbed truck, or if we stopped at the DQ as a family to get Peanut Buster Bar parfaits or chocolate dipped cones that we ordered at the small, screen windows that were, at the time, higher than my little head. As the DQ employee passed yummy treats to us through the same small, screen windows, it all seemed sweeter when my dad was along.

Richard never seems to meet a stranger. Although innately somewhat shy, he can talk to anyone easily. He will ask a couple of standard questions to any person he meets:

First, "Where you from? Where's your home, home…home?" Or "What's your middle name?" He can strike up a conversation easily with any Tom, Dick or Harry on the street by commenting on their pick-up truck or motorcycle! Or perhaps he'll mention the cap they're wearing or appreciate the little one that's riding in the stroller they're pushing. No matter what the comment, he makes an instant connection with his warm voice, friendly smile, or brief inquiry. Later he leaves behind a person, no longer a stranger but an acquaintance or friend. I've witnessed this thousands of times. He is masterful!

My dad seems to know everyone. In fact, when I was younger, I thought every cashier who was female, had the name Frida. Because he would greet each young lady with, "Well, Hello Frida!" It never occurred to me, until much later, that's just what he affectionately called each of them.

My Father, Richard has never been overly affectionate or super cuddly. But he lets me sit near him and pats me on the back. And he does give me hugs. Sometimes he gives this kind... squeezing so tightly he momentarily lifts me so that my feet dangle. This even though he is in his 80s. While squeezing, he'll often say, "Yep, I love you Rach!" as he pats me boldly three times. Smack, smack, smack. Or he'll give me a side hug pulling me near with his left hand while he shakes mine with his right, he looks me in the eye and blurts, "Good job!" I always savor those words because he means them. He's very encouraging, yet reserves those words for times when he's truly proud of me and because of that they have weight and a profound impact on me.

My Dad is an artist and always talked about his love for the genuine article. He likes things that are made from real leather, wood, glass, metal and stone. Things that look like what they are. He calls it, honesty of materials, one hundred percent pure. I grew up with driftwood and stones and gnarly branches and weeds cut from the ditch in a vase all as home decor. To this day, I love weavings and wooden boxes and sculptures and paintings and drawings.

My father also comments on people that he meets. As he gets to know them he'll say, "Now, that's the genuine article, the real McCoy!" I'm not even sure what that means, but I know he is speaking about real, authentic, true to who they are people. He is drawn to them. So am I. I'm glad that he vicariously taught me to look for that in people. Because of that, I can sense if something is a bit off or if someone is hiding, just pretending or even covering up in some manner. Richard Heggen is the real deal, the genuine article. What you see is what you get. When you get him - You know what you've got.

My dad is a storyteller. He always has a story to tell about his boyhood spent on the Iowa farm with his seven siblings, his life lessons, his random, almost unreal experiences, so strange that you know it's true because no one can make that kind of stuff up!

He has many stories from art school about some eccentric artist, his favorite professor or from his time spent teaching at Iowa State University. It may be a story or joke that he's recently heard and wants to share so he can laugh again. He's masterful at this too. We all have our favorite stories and request them as if standing at a jukebox selecting our favorite tune: B12 or J19. Even the grandkids, my nieces and nephews or my own children say, "Grandpa tell the one about…"

I have had the privilege for the duration of about ten years to teach summer art classes with my dad in Iowa. The truth is, I collected the money for graduate credit, took attendance, visited with all the teachers who were now the students and helped in clerical ways. Let it never be mistaken, my dad was teaching the class! And every teacher in Iowa that attended, whether to further their understanding, gain graduate credit or to renew their certification, each one gathered from Richard's rich wealth of art and design information and soaked it up like a dry sponge in fresh rainwater.

During those classes, I heard some of his stories repeatedly but never grew tired of hearing them. Each varying in duration, some disturbing, others touching, some are funny and my dad laughs while telling them. I would always wonder, as he was winding around the story looping it here and taking it there, was he going to come back to his point? Sometimes, I thought he'd forgotten a section or left out a particular detail, but then he would provide it specifically with the exact same inflection as before because it was a true story with vivid memories attached to each detail. But every time he would bring it to the conclusion: sometimes in full-circle manner and tying up all the loose ends or giving the moral of the story landing each brilliantly like a pilot who effortlessly touches the plane's wheels gently on the runway. I'd sit dumbfounded, shaking my head with the corners of my mouth turned upward in a soft smile, thinking to myself, *Man, he's done it again!* I was so proud to be his daughter and get to listen to him instruct, encourage and entertain.

I love to tell stories, too. People have told me I'm good at it. I know I've learned and been influenced by my Dad. In a sense I've taken master classes from a master without needing any art graduate credit.

My dad's love has helped me develop a strong sense of identity. I think I have always known who I was because I knew whose I was. I am Rachel, Richard Heggen's daughter. I think that's true spiritually as well. We can't know who we are until we know whose we are. We are our heavenly Father's: Created by, designed for, loved eternally, purchased forever and delighted in immeasurably by him. Although we all go through stages and phases, it's very important to know who we are deep down inside. My dad has always applauded the things that he has seen in me that are good. Every time I headed out the door as a young lady, his parting words would be, "Be good!" I don't think I realized how profound that was until I became older and wiser. In a world that is obsessed with looking good, it is important that we are asked and reminded to *be* good.

I remember asking my father as he stood on the back patio grilling pork chops about my outfit or my hairstyle or something. He said something like, "Rachel you could dye your hair purple, *this was long before anyone actually did* and people would think that's exactly the way you meant it to be, because you're a confident young lady. You are a Hot Dog! A Baggage Chief! Remember, some people don't like a Hot Dog but that's okay, you know who you are!"

My dad wasn't giving a lesson about food choices or meat. He called me a Hot Dog equating that with confidence. He was instilling in me a deep rooted confidence that doesn't waver due to people's opinion or become crushed by peer pressure or the desire to be popular or well liked. He loved me. He approved of me. That's what truly counted. Even to this day, that grounds me. The thought of this deep love makes my eyes drip with hot tears that stream down my cheeks even now!

Thank you, God, for my Dad.

I know some people are very confused and thoroughly messed up about God's love for them based on the pathetic example of an earthly father in their lives. This truly grieves me. But it doesn't make me ashamed or want to shy away from the overflowing and grateful heart I have for my earthly *and* heavenly father. I am not ashamed to testify about this goodness in my life because its source is Jesus. Every good and perfect gift comes from above. Everything good comes from Jesus. I know that! Undeserved yes, yet granted to me!

Backdrop to this Book:

Identity is defined: the condition of being oneself, and not another. BELOVED believer this is key.

So what's the story behind this book? Many years ago, I began to give a talk on our identity in Christ. It was called: *Is Your Identity in Crisis or in Christ?* I found that as I began to grasp my true identity to a greater degree, I gave this talk almost exclusively! I would steer the people inviting me to speak for events or retreats in that direction. I'd say, "Well, I have a talk on Identity in Christ that would be great and I'd love to come share it with your group."

Don't despise the day of small beginnings. I see now that God used a talk I first gave at retreats, decades ago, to solidify my own identity and He wooed me into his thoughts and heart about me. This brought a strong conviction through time spent with Him in the word. I couldn't contain myself and wanted to help free people in anyway I could by presenting, in any form, truths that might shift perspectives and loosen chains that lies have created or dismantle any law-based religious mindset.

If I can help or encourage anyone who may not know who they are in Christ, or just needs a different voice for the truths to be communicated, then I'm the gal and I'll raise my hand metaphorically speaking, and say, "I'm in!"

As the engagements continued to roll in, I'd percolate with excitement each time I had the opportunity to communicate to His beloved about their identity. I do realize a plethora of books have been written about IDENTITY IN CHRIST. I'm grateful for each one yet I still felt invited into the space because I've been given a voice and I had something to offer and share with my audiences and my sphere of influence.

I later realized I could have a greater reach, through a book, to touch people I may never have the privilege to stand before in one of my live audiences. So, if God uses me to help bring a greater number of people to His freedom plan through this book, again I'll say loudly, **"I'm in!"**

You, dear reader are not reading this book randomly or on a whim, this is a divine appointment. I've been praying for you and I'm grateful to share anything that may encourage you in your identity.

Bless you,
Rachel

Chapter One
Twenty Questions Game

I'd like to write about who/what we are not! Because it may clear somethings up for you. When I was young we played a game called, Twenty Questions. Have you ever played it? One person thinks of an item and the others try to guess the item by asking up to twenty questions.

When playing the Twenty Questions game, the first questions asked was, "Is it bigger than a bread box?" We don't often have bread boxes any more but it was commonly asked as a way to start. If the answer was yes then you guessed things that are bigger; if the answer was no you would think of items smaller than a bread box and the guessing game continued.

The reason I mention this is because, when it comes to our identity, it is as important to know who or what you ARE NOT as it is to know who or what you are. If you are a believer in Jesus Christ and He is your Savior and Lord, **you must know what you are NOT.** So, how about you start by saying these aloud.

I AM NOT:

- A sinner
- An orphan
- Judged by my past
- Loved because of my behavior
- Striving to reach God
- Disqualified
- Satan's prey (*the devil touches him not* - 1 John 5:18)
- The object of God's anger - Isaiah 54:9
- Able to save myself
- Anyone's savior - I give up my messiah complex

- Separated from God's love.
- Alone
- Big enough to mess up God's plans for my life.

This is just a start of a list of who you ARE NOT. If you'd like, now that you've read this list, repeat the list aloud as declarations. It is helpful to declare aloud the flip-side of these, the opposite, and we will get to that later.

Chapter Two
Instant Download

I received this next chapter from the LORD while I was visiting Redding, CA. It came in ONE chunk. I felt like He just deposited it into my spirit, BOOM! It came just a few weeks before as I was slated to speak at a prayer intensive to a group of people graduating from a Chaplaincy program. At the time of first writing this, both of my parents were still living and the information reflects their ages at the time. I've chosen to include this and **present it exactly the way I received it** that morning while staying in California.

You may not be a Chaplain but the information fits any believer so here's what I heard:

I know who I am! This is the message of the believer! I know who I am and I know whose I am. Who am I? That's the question of the world and what they are asking.

When you walk into a hospital room or the home of one of the people you are ministering to, you usher in the presence of God. You are light! Jesus said, "I am the light of the world!" Then He turned to his disciples and said, "You are the light of the world!"

If the people you are sent to don't know Jesus, you get to represent him. I heard a pastor say, RE-PRESENT him. Do that. And if they know Jesus you get to remind them of who *they* are in Christ.

Isaiah 62:4 NIV *"No longer will they call you Deserted, or name your land Desolate. But you will be called Hephzibah, and your land Beulah; for the Lord will take delight in you, and your land will be married."*

So...When I go to the post office I bring Jesus Christ, God the Father and Holy Spirit with me. Why? Because that's who I house. I am in Christ and **Christ is in me**.

In the Natural:

- I am the daughter of two 87 year old Iowans who have loved each other well and loved me beyond my wildest imagination.
- I am the 4th girl in a family of all girls...you got it right, I am the baby.
- I am married for 33 years to Michael, the most decent man on the planet and one who, as my former pastor Stuart Briscoe says, "makes me radiant!"
- I have three children Michael, Andrew and Grace who have given me a huge purpose while they were under our roof and a reason to pray now as they've flown our nest. The pain of my parenting and family situation is the reason I now am more aware from my role in the kingdom to exhort believers to know who they are in Christ.
- I am an author who could NOT read as a child. Seriously, I could NOT read nor could I spell.
- I was not a great test taker in school but was always on the dean's list at the University of Northern Iowa.

That's a bit of who I am in the natural!

Now are you ready? I want to tell you who I am in the spiritual. Who I am in Christ:

- I am a child of the Most High God
- I am accepted in the beloved.
- I am a saint!
- I am righteous.
- I am surrounded with favor.
- I am royalty.
- I am a royal priesthood a holy nation. I am a person belonging to God.
- I am an overcomer who overcomes and overcomes and overcomes until I look back and I can SAY, "I am more than a conqueror!"
- I am walking in the kingdom way.
- I am under the blood of Jesus
- My home is Heaven.
- I am called to bring Heaven to Earth...because I carry my Father, God's DNA. "On earth as it is in Heaven"
- I have deep humility but high confidence because God the Father has chosen me.

We must know who we are and whose we are! You see the wounded world is not looking for others to bump around in the dark with them, they are looking for light.

You are the light of the world SO SHINE! As you minister, you release what you carry!

The world isn't looking for other broken people to hang out with. They have already done that. They are looking for something different they want to experience wholeness and victory!

I'm sure you've heard this phrase, please know, it's a Biblical impossibility.

"I'm just a sinner saved by grace!" Yep! It's a popular song lyric. I'm sure you've heard this phrase many times. But as Pastor Pete Briscoe says, "It's a Biblical impossibility."

I WAS a sinner, now I'm saved by grace. Yay! God!

NOW I AM A SAINT!

"Jesus, Jesus, Jesus there's just something about that name. MASTER SAVIOR JESUS let all Heaven and Earth proclaim. Kings and kingdoms will all pass away BUT there's something about that name." That is the truth.

"He has ***rescued*** *us from the dominion of darkness and* ***brought*** *us into the kingdom of the Son he loves, in whom we have redemption, the forgiveness of sins."* Colossians1:13-14 NIV. Emphasis mine

"Therefore, IF anyone is IN Christ, he is a NEW creation. The old has passed away; BEHOLD, the new has come!" 2 Corinthians 5:17 ESV Emphasis mine.

What has happened to the old? It has passed away. My grandmother passed away when I was a young mom she lived a LONG life of almost 99 years. But she passed away. She no longer visited me and I no longer visited her because she had "passed away." That euphemism means, she died, she is dead! Because she has passed away it means she will no longer be an active force in my life.

YET, I have seen how we teach people their SIN will always visit them for the **rest of their life**. Because we say we're sinners!

BUT it is not true. If you know Jesus and are a believer, you are a saint. Your OLD nature has passed away! You no longer have a sin nature. You are a saint. You are a righteous, holy and blameless one.

You *may* have a sin habit BUT habits can be broken and you have inside of you, as Scripture says the Holy Spirit and he gives us the power NOT to sin. *"But I say, walk by the spirit, and you will not gratify the desires of the flesh."* Galatians 5:16.

If you are in Christ today, know this. You no longer have a sin nature! You have a NEW nature! Your spirit has been reborn. It's called sanctification. **Good news flash**: You are more PRONE to righteousness than you are prone to sin!

As Pete Briscoe said in a devotional, *Ying and Yang, good dogs and bad dogs, the force and its dark side. I'm telling you, the Christianized version of Taoism isn't just wrong; it sets our minds on the wrong thing. Think about it: if we are constantly worried about some sort of battle going on inside of us we're constantly focusing on ourselves, right?*

Our thoughts sound like this:
- *I can't give in!*
- *I have to win this war that rages within me.*
- *I have to get my act together.*
- *I have to suppress the bad part of me so that the good part of me can show Jesus.*
- *Jesus, help me!*

Sure, this looks pretty pious on the outside, but in reality, we have been tricked into a self-centered struggle to try to do what is right, rather than a Christ-centered celebration of what he has already accomplished on the cross.

You have to know who you are and more importantly, whose you are. It's time to own what has already been won, by Jesus Christ, for you.

You are a royal priesthood, own it! Because false humility manifests as if being humble says, "No, no, no I'm really nothing, just a weak sinful worm." But false humility is killing the Church and no one wants what we have!

Jesus paid much too high a price for us to not fully own, claim and walk in the newness of life he gave us. I believe Jesus should get his full reward and everything he died to give us. We must believe, embrace and live. We exalt Jesus Christ when we step into what he paid such a high price to purchase for us, our identity in him!

Chapter Three
It's a Family Affair

I am delighted to have parents who have prayed for me my entire life. They also pray for me when they know I am standing before an audience. I also have a team of people who pray for me. So know that you have been prayed for if you've been at an event where I have spoken. And even as I write, there's a team of people who are praying for me as well as the people that my messages reach. That's you!

My parents are both of Swedish dissent, not stoic but not overly emotional or demonstrative either. However, I seem to hug everyone around so if people don't wanna hug from me they need to give me *the signal* — the stiff arm. My dad, passed away at the end of 2020. Man, oh, man I miss him! I'm telling you, he was hilarious and such a gifted artist and master storyteller! My mom is very kind, beautiful and orderly and is a huge prayer warrior in my life. I tell you that because where you come from and who you are matters. When it comes to identity we need to know who we are and whose we are. It is key. So when you know your father, God, his ways, his character and his word, it is a game changer!

I love family! It is paramount to me! I love my parents and three sisters and their families tons and bunches. I'm so thankful for my husband and three children. I am blessed beyond measure and I know it. I take photos of everybody and project them onto screens when I go to speak because *my peeps* are the most' important thing to me and my greatest privilege in life and I want to share them. I think it is distinctive because family is the heartbeat of God. He refers to himself as Father and we are his children! I have children that live near and far and I'm grateful for getting to be their mom. Each one relates to me differently and I'm impacted greatly and I'm so thankful.

Each of my children have a special role in our family and it's interesting the way it plays out. We live quite close to our oldest, the middle one lives out in California and our daughter has lived in Michigan for years. I'm amazed by them, each one and the people God has designed them to be. I'm utterly tickled yet baffled at how children can all grow up in the same environment and be so different. I think God has such a unique design and stamp on each person from the beginning of their life. We were fashioned before the foundation of the world.

The things we go through as parents shows us the love God has for us, his kids. I know that my relationship with each of my children has helped form and fashion me more into who God wants me to be. He reveals his heart for me through the way I relate to my own children.

The enemy has tried to come against me BIG TIME, related to my family. He has hit hard hoping to silence me and discourage me or make me doubt God's goodness, but I have something to say and I will not be silenced. Often he has tried to stop me from giving messages to live audiences or from writing blog posts or books.

I believe the enemy took an arrow, aimed, then shot it directly at our family, but I know God is more powerful and intends to turn it around and make the enemy pay double. Good will come out of any difficult situation, because God is good and a powerful redeemer! He will use all things for his purposes and glory. I believe it, I believe it, I believe it and I'm living proof of it!

I can't wait to see all the ways God will use the hard things my family's experienced for his glory, my good, and ultimately the good of others in my life.

So, if you are going through something difficult, confusing and/ or painful in your family right now whether it be a strained relationship, estrangement, a prodigal child, or something just being "off." I'd like to say, I get it, I relate and I'm sorry, run to Jesus! I'd also like to pray for you right now, before I continue writing.

Father, your plan is unity! Your plan is never separation. You are a God who reconciles and restores, you make a way, so we don't know the way for these difficult or estranged relationships to come together but you're a way-maker, I declare it, in the name of Jesus. And God we don't understand but you understand everything! And even though the enemy may think strife will always mark our homes, it will not! We declare in the name of Jesus you're a restorer, you're a redeemer, you're a unifier, and we believe everything Jesus paid for is going to touch our families so we receive it now, in the name of Jesus, amen!

Some things are hard, right? Life is hard but don't get it confused; life is the thing that is hard but God is good. He's good, He's good He's good!

Before I go any further in this book, I want to give a shout out to my husband, Michael. He is the most easy-going man I've ever met. When I was in seventh grade we studied amoebas in science class. We put them on the slide, then beneath the microscope and the amoeba only moved when it got too hot. He's a great deal like that: easy going, amiable, my *Steady Eddie* and forerunner.

Michael rarely gets upset. Well, except for sometimes in traffic. Okay, I'm not joking, he is just the most laid-back, calm guy and he has few words. He fits perfectly with me! It's like God knew what he was doing, duh! Because I rattle on and on then pause and I ask Michael, "What are ya thinking about?" He says, "Nothing, I just like to hear your voice!" What? Every "Chatty Cathy" needs a guy like that. He's amazing, truly!

I have sisters three older sisters, no brothers, it's just us four girls: Barb, Sharon, Joyce and Rachel. One of my favorite photos of all of us is from a shopping spree down in Des Moines, Iowa. I keep it visible in my house because we had a wonderful day together and it captured such unity. Even though we have very different personalities we are all cut from the same cloth and we are for each other. On that day we saw a large sign in a shop window, it read SISTERS, it was the name of the little boutique. We knew we needed to sit right underneath it and get our photo taken. We were all wearing denim and smiling. It was a beautiful fall day. It's a very special photograph to me because these are the women in my life that I look up to. I honor them, they are funny, strong, compassionate and amazing! I am the baby and I love my place in the family! I love my place of last born; they take such good care of my parents and such good care of me. I'm telling you this because I often share stories about my upbringing and it may even come up in this book, who knows!

I absolutely love to tell "Barb Stories" and share them often with my audiences and I'll share some in this book too. Barb talks very deliberately and slowly and emphatically. She is a hoot! I often pray for her and I wanna just take a second to pray for you as well. Even though you've just begun to read this book, I'd like to say a prayer over you.

Father, I thank you for this person. I thank you that you love her with an everlasting love. Thank you for the beauty and poise and the story that you've placed in this dear one. Thank you that your plans for this reader are good, you give each one a future and a hope.

God, whatever is going on around her, I ask, right now, that you would bubble wrap her now. I thank you that you tell us that you are the shield around us and the lifter of our heads. So whatever we go through in life you're going to bubble wrap us in transit, and I thank you.

Lord, you know this one's name, you made her and wired her and I bless her from the top of her head to the soles of her feet. I pray you give her rest at night. You say, "I will lie down and sleep in peace, not in pieces, for you're the one that makes me dwell in safety." Bless her Holy Spirit and read this book to her, in the name of Jesus, amen.

I'd like to share two stories and ask three questions over the next few chapters. It's important to note that both my husband and our eldest son, are named Michael. It gets confusing at times so if you happen to be pregnant reading this book my FREE unsolicited advice is don't!

Chapter 4
Tooth Fairy and Identity

We homeschooled all three of our children, I don't mention it for a badge, it's just the truth. One day, Michael went out to play in the neighbor's sandbox. We lived in the Minneapolis area at the time and he went out with his younger brother, Andrew and he had his tooth that he had recently lost too. He was all excited about the tooth fairy, and he had the tooth in a little Tupperware cup. It was a short container smaller than a sippy cup.

I have no idea why he went out to the sandbox with the container that held his tooth. I have no idea why his MOTHER let him go out to the sandbox with said tooth, but he went out there! And it, well…he lost it!

So he came inside for school and we were about to do some writing. Long ago kids used paper, do you know what that is? The top section had a place to illustrate something and below it were ruled lines to write the story and practice penmanship.

Michael was so upset because he had lost his tooth and his brother, three years younger, was the one who had done something that caused it. He was so upset and I said, "Michael, here's what we're gonna do, during writing class you can tell me the whole story and I'll dictate everything you say. You can make a crayon drawing and then we will submit your paper to the tooth fairy so she will still give you your money." So we did that! And it worked out great!

I knew we were getting somewhere in our homeschool because Michael sat down and he told me the story. He said, "Andrew lost the tooth and I was tempted to hit him, but I gain self-control!"

I was so excited, I almost dropped my pen. I wanted to scream and run around the school table where we were seated. Yay! Michael knew self-control is to control one's self without some outside force doing it. I felt we were making headway in teaching and learning. So we wrote the story/note together and I planned to put it under his pillow at night, have dad pay him the tooth fairy fee and we'd be all good. My plan worked like a dream!

But the second time he lost a tooth we simply stuck the tooth under his pillow without placing any money. He woke up in the morning and he came directly into my room. My husband had already left by this time to go to work.

Michael came in to our master bedroom and he had little Iowa State Cyclones pajamas on. He was the cutest little guy. He had tears shooting, like fireworks, straight out of his eyes and he began to blubber and said, "Mommy, this time I **had** the tooth! But the tooth fairy didn't leave," he broke down crying and through broken speech continued, "Meeee aaaaany m- - - oooo-ney!"

I thought, *oh my word, who is it that forgot to put the money under his pillow? Me! Oh, no what am I gonna do? You're such a loser mom!* I try not to adopt that lie, of being a loser but I must admit I thought it. *I've got to do something!* You know what I did? Quickly, I mean it embarrasses me how quickly, lies started tumbling out of my mouth!

And I said, "Michael, you know what? Sometimes the tooth fairy has to send a substitute. Did you know mommy used to teach in the public school system? Well, before I did, I was a substitute teacher! A substitute tries very hard to do the same things the teacher would do but she may still do things a little differently. Maybe the tooth fairy sent a substitute!"

Lie! Lie! Lie! The lies were just bursting out of my mouth like water from a fire-hydrant. I wasn't lying about being a substitute, that part's true, but I was lying to my child about the tooth fairy.

"Listen, son, why don't you go back into your room again because maybe the tooth fairy sent a substitute and she may have placed the money by the door, or maybe it's on the ledge of the window, or look again under your pillow. You could even check underneath the bed. Did you try that?"

I just needed him to get out of the bedroom! In that particular house we had a recessed shelving area in our master bedroom. And Michael, my husband, had a place where he kept his keys in a container and he kept loose change there also. I thought *as soon as my son leaves, I'm going to take some coins and I'll stick them under daddy Michael's pillow.*

You see, I'm pretty sure I mentioned earlier, I have both a husband and a son named Michael. And I thought, if I stick this under the pillow I will fake my child out. So I stuck the money under my husband Michael's pillow and my son came back in, really distraught this time.

He moaned, "Mom I checked by the window, I looked under the bed, and there is NO money. I don't know if the tooth fairy sent a substitu…"

I interrupted him, "Michael," I said, "I am so sorry that happened to you, son we will try to figure it out. How about if we just make the beds for now and get on with our day. Okay? Why don't you fluff dad's pillow. You get on dad's side of the bed and I'll be here on mine."

We both tugged the covers and I knew what was about to happen, because I had shoved all the coins under my husbands pillow!

Next, little Michael fluffed the pillow as I fluffed mine, just mirroring what I was doing and as I was fluffing mine, I heard him gasp, “Mom! There’s a bunch of money under dad’s pillow! What is going on?”

And I said through laughter, “Oh, the tooth fairy probably did send a substitute. And the tooth fairy’s substitute doesn’t know whether it’s **young** Michael or **daddy** Michael, that silly tooth fairy! I don’t know what happened, but just take the money, it must be for you!”

So here’s the deal, that is one important thing you must understand because it relates to our identity and what we believe and what we make agreements with as well. You see, he bought the lie, little Michael bought it because it came from somebody he trusted, me!

We all have lies coming at us all the time. But the thing is, a lie in and of itself is no big deal. It has no power. The lie actually falls flat. It’s when we partner with a lie, that we empower the liar. I think that’s a Bill Johnson quote, “When you believe a lie, you empower the liar.”

Let me add this because it may further illustrate my point. It’s a quick story about when our second son Andrew first lost a tooth. I will never forget it, our three children were seated at the kitchen bar and I was serving them cut up apples with peanut butter and cinnamon.

Now our oldest, Michael came out of my womb a bit like Alex P. Keaton from the sit-com, carrying a little briefcase, logical and very articulate! He instructed his brother Andrew in a very directive manner, "Now Andrew, I need you to keep your tooth very safe!"

Andrew responded, "Okay!"

Michael continued, "And just so you know, the tooth fairy could send a substitute!"

You might be able to see, not only had Michael adopted the lie but he had now, perpetuated it! **I told you I'd share two stories and ask three questions.** But before I move on from this tooth fairy story, I hope you understand this has a lot to do with identity. Sure, we have all received some lies along the way, but it's when we've adopted and partnered and made agreements with them that we empower the liar. And quite possibly we've passed these lies on to other people.

Chapter 5
Get Unstuck

Here is a quick Barb story. Like my dad did, she often wears a cap. And on this particular occasion she was wearing a little black wool cap the day we were traveling to my uncle's funeral. I was in Iowa already, but we needed to travel a little further north. Michael and I were staying at my sister Sharon's farm house and I wanted even more "sister time."

So to maximize my sister time, I proposed an idea to them on the phone, "Why don't you guys come to the farm with mom and dad, then get in our car and we can travel to the funeral together. That way, I'll have more time with you Joyce and Barb and we can chat as we travel. Michael will just drive us all like, *driving Miss Daisy*, and he'll take us where we need to go!"

They agreed, so that was our plan. My sisters, Joyce and Barb would first be traveling with my parents, then head north up to the farm, and we'd go together from there.

You need to know something about my dad, he was an amazing, amazing man! Yet the truth is, he used to get a little nervous at times. He'd get a little, "hept up," as we call it. I mean he was wound up because we had an appointed time to be somewhere and a destination to be at, combined that with the inclement weather that day and… Oh, Boy! So yeah, my dad was a little hept-up.

Those of you who know me, or maybe you've guessed, I'm a wee bit like him! Well, yeah! He was a little charged up, so Barb was getting the overall hept-up"vibe" in the car, as little bit of anxiety was brewing.

Barb came dashing out of my parents' car and wanted to rush into our car as quickly as possible. Probably my dad had said something like, "Hop out of the car, go! We need to get up there on time."

So Barb got out of my parents' car same as Joyce, and flew toward my vehicle and she sat down, but she did not shut the car door. She was in the backseat and she was kind of in a strange position with her legs still dangling out. She was seated and she threw her head back, and she said, "Oh Rach! I suppose you're gonna tell THIS one!"

Now, here's the deal, Barb knows that I often tell "BARB" stories. She has given me carte blanche permission to tell Barb stories, she's never signed a contract but she did agree I could tell stories at speaking engagements. However, her one caveat was, and these are her words, "Just let people know; make sure they know I'm a relatively intelligent person!"

She thought, *I'm sure Rachel's going to tell this story to people.* And she loudly whined, "Oh Rach, I suppose you're going to tell this one!"

Meanwhile, I was seated in the front seat next to Michael and I turned to look in the backseat and I said, "Barb I don't even know what it is yet, how can I know whether I will tell it."

She voiced a slow sustained complaint, "I'm stuck!"

"What?" I asked.

Barb repeated, "I'm SSSTTUUUCK! My tights are stuck!"

You see it a hurry to please our Dad she had caused quite a situation that she was now stuck in.
Let me help you picture it. She had a black sweater and a black skirt, and she had her little a pair of paisley, fish-net type tights on and what happened was she had on zip-up, high black boots. The little zipper fob had connected to the thread on her fish-net tights. She basically, had crocheted herself into a very strange position.

So she was delayed there with her legs stuck together in the backseat and she didn't even shut the door and it was cold outside.

But she shouting, "I'mmmmmm stuck!"

Now, my sister Joyce, she's the middle one, she's the one who cares for the nomads, she will give them food, she will give them a carry-out bag, she basically takes care of EVERYONE'S needs!

So quickly, Joyce got her little glasses out of her purse and said, "Barb! Hang on, let me get you UNSTUCK."

So she looked through her readers and begins to remove…

Now, I meanwhile, was in the front seat, Michael was about to take off and I was sitting shotgun. I looked at Barb and I was thinking, *I hope that works out for you!* Because I'm the baby! And you know the baby doesn't do much, they just hope it all works out. Just being honest…

In my case, while I was thinking, *Well I hope that works out for you!* Joyce was over there helping and she got Barb settled down and she found where the little piece of thread was attached to the zipper fob and she got Barb's tights unstuck! YAY!

All the while, I'm thinking… *Barb! Those tights are fish-net, you could've just pulled your legs apart and snapped the threads, nobody would've even known!*

Barb sighed and exclaimed, "Oh, I'm so glad, thank you, Joyce because I thought it was going to have to walk like a mermaid to the uncle Don's funeral!"

Here's the reason I write the story about Barb's tights getting stuck. It's because I think it has a lot to do with our identity and who we are in Christ and how we view things. We can be in a hurry to please the father and get stuck along the way. We have to get out of the mindset that we are being sternly watched and we are pressed to please Him or else.

You see, one of the reasons I'm on the planet, is to get rocks out of the road for people so they can go down the way that God wants them to go. And I think sometimes I'm just here, maybe it's today as you read this, to get somebody's tights UNSTUCK, the tights of your thinking or of your believing.

Here's where you may easily have gotten your tights stuck. It can happen to any of us. We can be in this Christian life thing where we think we've got to please the father, we've got to please the father, we've got to pleas… do whatever God wants us to do, hurry, hurry, hurry because he's gonna get mad at us if we don't.

And so we rush around in this, Christian life thing and we just get, doggone STUCK! You see that's what happened to Barb. It can happen easily. We can be in a hurry and find ourselves striving to please the Father it is works-based and law-based.

I'm gonna raise my hand. Mine is held up high. Raise your hand, metaphorically speaking, as I ask you this Question: **In your**

Christian journey, have you ever been stuck? Perhaps you've thought, *I've got to please God, I've got to please God, I've got to do certain things a certain way to be accepted or approved or even liked?* Have you felt that way? Or have you thought, *I have to earn the Father's love?*

Because here's the truth, if you were to picture father, God's face right now, no one has seen God face-to-face, but if you were to picture his countenance, his face as he looks at you, can you picture it? What is his face doing? Now close your eyes, right now picture it and PAUSE. WAITING… Seriously, close your eyes, what would his face be doing?

Open your eyes!

Let me reassure you. He is smiling at you! Yes, He is smiling at you. He is delighted he made you! He knows who you are, He has great plans for you. No, He is not stern, glaring at you thinking *you better figure this out! Do you know that I'm watching you girl? You better please me!*

In Scripture we see the way God acts towards his people. *God blesses you; He rises to show you compassion.* It says in Psalm 103, *He knows how we are formed, he remembers that we are dust.* Because he created us. It also says in Numbers 6, *He lifts up his countenance upon us, he smiles upon you and gives you peace.*

Maybe you've believed a lie and you think God is mad at you. He's not! *His anger lasts only a moment,* it says in Scripture, ***but his favor last a lifetime!*** Right? So we've got to get UNSTUCK! The reason I mention it is because I know it can happen to anyone. No shame, just recognize it if that's what you're thinking and believing.

I'm here to write and remind you: you are LOVED! You get to be loved. Also I want to alert you as a warning that a religious Spirit might rise up anytime someone starts telling you about God's love and grace. I'm here to write and remind you of the truth. You are loved and God is not mad at you and you don't have to strive and work to be loved, God's love is free and it's available.

I'm not talking about what some people call cheap grace, no it was bought with high price, the precious blood of Jesus Christ. It is not cheap. But I am all about applying the blood of Jesus Christ, and all that it bought for us, does that make sense?

So some of us just need to get our tights **unstuck**, okay? It's a vitally important thing! You've got to know, accept and believe how precious you are to your Father, God. That needs to be settled. It is key to secured identity! He is for you. He is not mad at you. His smile is upon you. He sings over you at night. He goes before you and behind you and making your way straight.

I told you I was going to ask you a few questions: **Whose view do you have of yourself?**

Is it the view that God has of you? He's saying, *I made you, I've designed you. You're a masterpiece and I'm smiling at you.* Whose view do you have of yourself and...

Whose voice are you listening to? You see, we all have voices in our head. Yes, we hear voices. Maybe a voice says, *you're junk,* *nobody likes you. No one cares about you!* That's a straight up lie. So let me ask again, whose view do you do have of yourself? Whose voice are you listening to?

The third question is: **Is your identity in Crisis or in Christ?** I'm hoping to unpack this further in the following chapters. Is your identity in crisis or is it rooted in Christ?

Because if it's rooted in Christ, you know it and the world around you also knows it. It can be seen, even sensed and felt, and others will want what you have. That's why when our identity is secure we will be able to share with others about the hope we have in Jesus.

Chapter 6

What I Learned in Art Class

So whose view do you have of yourself? That is a biggie. If it's not God's view your eye-sight is a little wacky, just saying!

I told you that my father was an amazing man, an Iowan and before he retired, I would go to Iowa to teach with him. The truth is, I would keep a record of who signed up for graduate credit, take the attendance, collect the tuition and do clerical stuff but my dad, he was the master artist. He was amazing!

Richard, that was my dad, was also so funny. He would walk around the classroom and visit with students. He would take an X-Acto knife and use it to cut things out of the magazines people would bring in, he'd cut a piece from an Asian rug pictured in a magazine add, he cut a piece out with his X-Acto knife and he'd make himself a little necktie and would attach it to his collar and wear it around the classroom. He cracked me up!

The students, on the first day, would be thinking, *who is this guy?* And later they would realize he's kind of fun. He would take the eyeball from a DOVE soap ad of some woman model and cut it out with the X-Acto knife and paste it on the inside of his glasses. Then he'd walk around with one Richard Heggen eyeball and the other paper eyeball that looked kind of strange. People would be working on their water color paintings or working on their designs and they'd look up and be startled and freak out. I loved teaching with my dad.

I found a pair of wacky glasses one day and I bought two pairs. My dad and I wore them around the classroom together just to be goofy. I have worn them in front of so many audiences! I wear them because the eyes are a little off kilter and they are very, well… just disturbing.

But I wear them because they illustrate that my view could NEVER be correct. And so I would ask you again, Whose view do you have of yourself? Because if your view doesn't line up with what God says in Scripture then your view is off kilter as well.

Those wacky glasses make me think of my question about vision. Whose view do you have of yourself? If you don't have a view of what Scripture says about you then you will be a little off and that causes wacky vision and can easily lead to wacky beliefs too.

I've found the best prescription lens is the Bible, the word of God. It will correct your vision right now! Whose view do you have of yourself? Whose voice are you listening to? These two questions are asked because the answers form two foundational pillars that are so important in securing of our identity.

We all have a SELF-VIEW! I pray your view is not wacky.

We all hear voices and we all have a voice.

Wow! The power of our words is astounding! I heard a pastor/ prophet say, "If you want to change your scenery, change your sound." You see our words, create worlds.

It says in Proverbs 18:21 ESV *Death and life are in the power of the tongue, and those who love it will eat its fruits.*

Wow, what a huge contrast, life versus death. *The power of life and death is in the tongue and those who love it will eat its fruit.* In other words, our words create worlds. God said, let there be light! Light, light, light, light and God's word continues on. *The grass withers, and the flowers fall but the word of the Lord endures forever.*

Chapter 7

Wacky Glasses and Wax Lips

I was talking about the power of our words once to a retreat audience. I had earlier shared some of these same stories with them; the ones about teaching with my dad and the art room and cut out eyes and magazine neck ties, etc. I had just taken the stage for my final session that Saturday and as I began my introduction on the topic of the power of our words, I glanced at the front row.

Right smack in front of me was this group of 20 year-olds, about six of them and they were lovely, wonderful young women, just sitting in the front row, sweet little honey bunnies who came to this session on words. They sat with their heads down but, as if on queue, they all lifted their heads at the same time to reveal a surprise for me.

Each wore a pair of glasses with one paper eyeball cut out from a magazine. Plus each gal wore a pair of bright red wax lips. With heads cocked, they sat looking right at me, it was absolutely hilarious. The funky-eyed glasses and huge, red wax lips have been used forever to illustrate my point.

Remember, I had just started speaking about the power of our words because words create worlds and as I looked at them, I saw them elbowing each other and enjoying their humor. I busted out laughing. They wondered if I was mad. I said, "Are you kidding me? This is absolutely hilarious, so fun!"

I pointed at the lips and glasses and then asked one of them, "Where'd you get those wax lips?"

"Oh, we went into town during our break and we got these and treats."

"Where?" I inquired.

The brunette chimed in, "We went to the old-fashion candy store in town that sells necklaces, the beaded ones that you can eat until there is only a string of elastic and multiple other kinds of candy. We found these wax lips there and knew we had to wear them tonight.

I know it was kind of gross that she had already worn and had them in her mouth, but I immediately asked, "Can have them?"

She stood up and reached her hand toward the stage and gave them to me! And I've been using them both ever sense. Wacky glasses and red wax lips. I keep them: glasses are for seeing and the lips remind me of voices, speaking and also listening.

I'll repeat my two questions again:

- **Whose view do you have of yourself?**
- **Whose voice are you listening to?**

There will always be a voice in your head, therefore you have to discern its source.

I want to turn a corner for a second as we go into voices. Yes, we all hear voices. It says in Scripture, "My sheep hear my voice, I know them, and they follow me." So there are voices and with those voices come these lies or truths.

We are bombarded, we have a God who loves us and an enemy who can't stand us. We have a God who is much more powerful, important and bigger than the enemy, but the enemy is there.

So when it comes to voices, consider four origins:

- An angel's
- Mine
- God's, the Holy Spirit
- The enemy's, the accuser, the Devil

So to keep the voices and sources straight, I think of it with words and motions: a voice could be the voice of an angel, we know that angels appear to people, we read about it in the Bible. And the angels talked. So it could be an angel. By the way, often times, the angel started by saying, "Fear not" because they were big or bright, intimidating creatures. The voice could be an angel. I'm not discounting that. Yes, it could be an angel, they still exist today.

There's another voice, point yourself and say… Me. The voice could be your own voice. You could have a voice in your head that says, "Don't forget to bring your keys this morning." That voice is just you and it's important to distinguish because people aren't sure whether they had a God thought or just a me thought.

And let me tell you, if you know Jesus Christ then the Spirit of God lives in you. When distinguishing voices, I think it's important that we turn a corner and say to ourselves, *by default it's probably God's voice, but it could be my own.* Many people live with it turned the other way around. We believe it's usually just me, but I guess it could be God. This flip needs to be made because we are spirit beings, new creations and we have the mind of Christ.

If you know Jesus, if you're in the Word, if the Spirit of God lives in you and because we have the mind of Christ, then the default setting may serve us better to think along these lines: ***Well, I'm a re-created being, a new creation who thinks the thoughts of God.***

When a thought or voice comes, especially when it seems out of nowhere, like you've rolled down the window of your being, so to speak, or when you're quiet and have enough time and a little bit more margin in your life because you've slowed down, then you hear the voice. When those thoughts/voices come in, ***it's from God***. I invite you to hug yourself, yes, right now! Give yourself a comforting hug because *the comforter* is the Holy Spirit. So it could be the voice of the Holy Spirit, the comforter, God's voice.

The voice could also be from an ungodly spirit. Let me explain why it's so easy to distinguish his voice. It's even fun for me to remind you of his dirty game and expose him because then his voice is no longer shrouded or disguised and you'll be more aware of his trick or schemes.

The enemy, the devil's voice is the voice of the accuser, so you will always feel, what? Accused! You will feel condemned. You will feel less than. You might feel like you messed up or it's all your fault. Do you understand? His voice is very easy to tell because it's as if he's wagging his finger at you! Recognize it. That is the voice of the accuser.

So a quick review on voices:

- An angel's
- Mine
- God's, the Holy Spirit
- The enemy's, the accuser, the Devil

I hope that makes sense to you. Let me just tell you, when it comes to lies we need to recognize their sound and how they've entered. I've mentioned this in my book He Speaks, but I think it is so foundational as it relates to our identity that I'm going to stress it here too. I like to think of it as ABC-D.

Perhaps you could use the whole alphabet but let me just give you these ABC-D's the source listed first as lies then from God:

A: Remember if you feel **A: Accused** it is from the accuser. It could be as simple as something as, *they asked you to make that cake that everybody loves but you ruined it! This time… you baked it too long, you can't even do simple things correctly*.

But if you feel **A: Affirmed** its God's voice. He says, *you go girl! I've made you and I love how you make a cake*. If you feel affirmed and loved and encouraged the voice is from God. *I made you!* Think about it, if you're a parent or grandparent when your child or grandchild messes up, you do not belittle them, you remind them "Hey, you will do better next time" because you know they can do it.

B: Let's go onto the **B: Belittled and Berated**. The voice is from the accuser. You've heard him, right? He picks at you, like a woodpecker on a tree. He picks at you and he is scolding and harsh. So, when you hear that voice, remember it is **not** from God and you have to reject it. You have to reject his voice right away. Don't listen, accept or partner with it, no way!

But if it is **B: Beloved** it is from God. Scripture calls you the beloved. We get to BE LOVED. Just be loved. **Listen, if you don't receive anything else I have written, please receive this. I'm writing to let you know God loves you!** He loves you! He loves you because he loves you. Just be loved. Yes, just be loved. Be the beloved in the beloved, Jesus Christ.

C: Let's go on to **C: Condemned.** The enemy wants you to think there's already been a trial by jury and the gavel has hit the judge's desk with the loud boom and you are condemned. You're guilty, you live in shame.

However, the **C: Confirmation, Compassion and Comfort** comes from God. The Holy Spirit is comforter, guide, friend and he comes close and near you. He is your helper.

It's very important for you to know these distinguishing differences in both the voice and tone and even how you feel after listening. Sure we can't base everything on feelings but we don't need to discount them either. Even when God disciplines us his correction is both loving and kind. *It's his kindness that leads us to repentance* it says in Scripture.

D: Now **D: Defective, Dumb, Defeated or Dread.** If the voice is from the enemy, he tries to paint your future with a spirit of dread.

BUT… If the voice is from God you are more aware and convinced that you are **D: Defended and Delivered and DEARLY loved.** You're delivered from all your sins and please know, you ARE dearly loved.

It's so important to understand that when lies come in, we have to combat them with the truth found in Scripture. We have to replace lies with the truth of God's word! The Word the Word, THE WORD! I can't stress that enough. We have to know what the word says, Jesus' actions, the character and nature of God and the sound of His voice because it all comes into play.

We know voices can come from different sources and we must recognize that. Once you recognize the voice, the scenarios may not even need to play out because once you know which voice you are listening to you can shut it down. We do not want to be in the enemy's camp any longer! We don't have to listen to his lying voice. We get to feast on the truth. Yippee! Yay! Yahoo! This is a game changer!

When the bogus lies come in. *Your sister could have done that better, your husband no longer loves you, you have a bleak future, you won't make it this month your money is going to run out, that pain in your body is…* Blah, Blah, Blah, Blah, BLAH! I don't even care what the lie is, but when it comes in it is crucial that you are able to recognize it.

That is your first defense, **you have to recognize the voice.** Once you recognize it, you've got to reject it immediately! It has no place in your thought life; it has no place in your dreams; it has no place in your future, you've got to reject it! Don't play around with it and wonder about it - REJECT it.

Remember, in Scripture it tells us we have the authority, how do we have the authority? We have the authority because Jesus gave it to us. All authority in heaven and on earth has been given to him. How much authority? All! All authority! He said all authority has been given to me. All authority in heaven and earth has been given to me therefore go and make disciples. He gives them (us) the authority to trample on snakes and cast out demons, etc.

Let me try to illustrate this regarding authority. I don't at present have the authority to do this, but because I'm 5' 2" I would love to be a police traffic guard for just a day. If I were given that authority, I think it would be fun.

I would relish the opportunity to have a Mack truck coming my way and only have to stick out my hand to make the driver stop. If I were directing traffic, I could blow my little silver whistle and tell certain people to go one way, but I could with my hand stiffly out-stretched, signal traffic to **STOP.**

And so it's like that when the lies come in, we must recognize it and then, if it's not confirmation and approval and if it's not about being his beloved and if it's not the voice of God, we reject it like it's a Mack truck trying to run us over. We must STOP it.

I want to illustrate how easily this can happen. I was giving this talk about identity once at a conference. I knew that God was using me and as I was getting ready to tell the ladies the reject part and was about to have them stick their hands out as if stopping a mac truck in traffic, guess what? I was hearing voices at the same time, and here's what I was hearing, *"You know they're not third graders, just because you used to teach elementary school kids does not mean that you have to treat these people like third-graders. Stop having these ladies do these silly hand motions."*

Seriously, I was doing the motions and was talking about doing it, it was happening to me. I was hearing the voice of the accuser. Guess what? I pushed through that voice because I knew God wants us to declare these things. So, I said, "Ladies if the voices of the enemy comes, you have to just reject it." I'll never forget it, I had my hand out as if stopping traffic with such fervor and passion demanding enemy get out of my head right now, I reject you!

A few days later I led a Bible study on a Tuesday that followed the Saturday's big conference and a sweet little 25-year-old friend said, "You know what Mrs. Inouye? I was in my apartment, I started to make something in my kitchen when the enemy kept coming at me with lies, *you know what you did in the past you will never be good enough or free from that.* And he was just attacking me as I was trying to make some blueberry muffins." She admitted, "I was standing in my kitchen and I was so thankful for Saturday's session because I just boldly said, 'I reject that!'" I think she even did the motions!

Listen readers if I had not pushed through at the conference and had believed the voice that was trying to stop me from speaking and showing my physical demonstrations of "REJECT," she may not have had breakthrough. We are here to equip. Iron sharpening iron, believers holding and linking arms together so we can go forward in the kingdom. Do you understand?

I know my role is to encourage you to know who you are and know whose you are. So you think I'm just telling you a little something helpful, but this is truth! So that when the enemy comes in and the voice makes you feel condemned, cruddy and shamed, it's not from God. Some of you, I can just feel are wondering, wait a minute, sometimes he corrects us and he gets after us. True, but how does he do it? What's his tone? *It's his kindness that leads us to repentance. Scripture says.*

Even when he corrects me and has to discipline me, it's the voice saying, *Honey I've got to tell you something, the way you spoke to her you need to make a phone call and you need to clean it up.* And if I don't clean it up or I delay the next day he does not tell me, *do you know how stupid you are? Do I have to tell you again?* No, he kindly says, *I want to remind you to make a phone call to make it right, cleanup on aisle 12.*

Yes, He'll even joke with me to get me to move. He tells me, yes of course he does and when he does, I feel the safety of him going with me to make right whatever needs to be made right. It says in 1 John 1:9 *If we confess our sins he is faithful and just to forgive us in and cleanse us from all unrighteousness.* He is a loving heavenly father.

So what happens, often times is, we get our tights stuck and we think we've got to do this, do this, do this, but we've got to recognize and reject! So let me review, because its vital and review helps. So let's do some motions together first, point to your temple. You've got to **recognize** the lie. Now put your hand out like you're stopping a Mack truck, AND **reject** it!

Here's the deal, you have to think differently or reconsider. It's called **repent**. RE: Again. PENT: at a higher level, change of mind like the penthouse, top-level, a higher view.

Turn toward the light, literally, it is a Greek word meaning "change of mind" repentance is necessary and valuable because it brings about a change of mind. It's not a one time thing but a continual process of turning away, in this case from the lies and turning to the truth.

For this **repent** motion, I'd like you to take your hands, place them near your head and raise them up like you're taking a hat off your head… It's the hat of all the cruddy and stinking thinking and all the lying voices and **RE-PENT.** You've got to think again on a higher level! You are basically taking that thought off and then I'd like you to simply admit yes, I partnered with this lie or thought. Maybe it was for just a day or for an hour or for 60 years. *I thought this about myself, or I believed this. But I* ***renounce*** *it!*

Just like you're ripping up a contract that you would not be willing to sign. *Nope, I will not think that thought again! Because it is not true, it is not what the blood of Jesus purchased for me. It's not what Jesus won on my behalf.* So you get to rip it up and **renounce** it. There is one more point I'd like to bring up and it holds the key. But I'm gonna review:

- Recognize
- Reject
- Repent
- Renounce
- __________

Let's practice, let's say a lie comes in. The lie may be: *You do not have a future and you should give up hope. And by the way, everybody in the world has a purpose but you.*

That is a lie!

I'm just curious, have you ever heard that lie? Well, I have! *Everybody in the world has a purpose but you.* Has that one ever come in? Probably yes…

So let's practice now, if/when you hear this lie: *"you know you don't really have a purpose and your future is not bright and God is not taking care of you, he's abandoned you."*

Immediately you need to gasp and take a deep breath in. It's now dawned on you, *it's a lie*, and point to your temple like you have a liberating thought, you **recognize** it!

Now get that same hand ready to stiff-arm that thought, you must **reject** it!

After you reject it, you're gonna touch your head because you're going to **repent**, think again on a higher level. **REPENT**! *(you are doing great I can feel you participating with me as you read. I think we might have 100% participation, I am so excited! This is going to be a really great day, I can feel you, as you process.)* Remember just as if you're taking something off like a horrible hat, lift it off and put your hands high.

And then, rip that contract up like you won't sign it and say renounce loudly. **Renounce!** And I'd like you to say it like you are fed up with that stuff and you will rip that contract up right now, in the name of Jesus!

So one, two, three shout, **RENOUNCE!** So, as your hands are here, above your head ripping things up, here's the last one, and you are sunk if you don't do this last one. Now take your hands and touch your head like you are putting new things into your brain and **replace**.

This is vital, guess why? Let's use a diet as an example. If you don't replace the shelf that the Twinkies used to be on, you would still eat Twinkies, OK! You have to replace the thoughts and lies with truth. Just as Matthew 12:44 warns, you have to fill your mind with truth so the enemy can't take it over again.

They all start with "R." Yes, that's purposeful. You are free to choose differently but please do the motions as you do these:

- Recognize
- Reject
- Repent
- Renounce
- **REPLACE**

We all know we have voices coming at you all the time. They could be from the Holy Spirit, they could be from you, they could be from an ungodly spirit, or an angel. But you have to **recognize, reject, repent, renounce, and replace.** I may be repeating them again and again because I want. Your brain to lock it in.

I used to sing to teach to my kids their states and capitals and other memorable facts. God even gave me a song to help cement these truths in my spirit. Obviously, I can't sing it to you here but you can make one up with the five "Rs" if you'd like.

I am hoping that these will never leave you. And that you will not be able to dump this out of your brain. If these keep repeating in your mind I'd be so grateful because I know that I know that I know who I am and I know that I know that I know whose I am. I know who I am and so I'm able to celebrate who I am and I honor and celebrate who you are. Each of you are getting just a little bit of my life's journey. I hope to take you on a journey that has helped me with my own identity.

> *"I can't afford to have a thought in my head about me that God doesn't have about me."* Pastor Bill Johnson

LIES must be replaced by TRUTH: ***I've listed some lies, then truth afterwards and in BOLD letters so let truth stick with you.***

- *I can't get it together*/Truth: **My whole spirit and soul and body is kept blameless**... God is faithful he is the one that will surely do it. (1 Thessalonians 5:23, 24)

- *God doesn't hear or listen to me*/Truth: **God invites me to call Him.** He will tell me about things I don't already know. And He will answer me while I'm speaking. (Jeremiah 33:3; Isaiah 65:24)

- *I should just give up*/I can't do this/Truth: **I will reap a harvest, if I don't give up!** (Galatians 6:9-10)

- *I'll never break free*/Truth: **The weapons I fight with are mighty** to pull down strongholds in anything raised against the knowledge of God. (2 Corinthians 10:3-5)

- *God doesn't love me. Or God loves me but not as much as someone else.* / Truth: God loves me and the world so much He sent Jesus, He sings over me at night, and **He loves me lavishly** and calls me his child! (John 3:16; Zephaniah 3:17; 1 John 3:1)

- *I am not whole, I'm junk/I'm not put together right, I'm nothing special!*/ Truth: **I am God's masterpiece, handiwork, poem,** created in Christ Jesus to do good works...what God has already prepared for me. I am made on purpose for a purpose! Ephesians 2:10.
- *I am too weak.* /Truth: **God's power is perfect in my weakness.** The Lord is my strength He makes my feet like the deer's; I tread on high places...I shall run and not be weary. (2 Corinthians 12:9-11; Habakkuk 3:19; Proverbs 21:30; Isaiah 40:28–31)

Emphasis mine.

Chapter 8
It's Time to Let Go

"It's time to let go." Wow! This is one of my favorite lines from the movie Top Gun-Maverick. The line is not spoken but it's written on a computer by the character, Ice Man who can no longer speak without difficulty so he types this line, "It's time to let go!"

Such good advice…it's time to let go! Yes, it fits for many situations, so many circumstances and a big chunk of life. Right? It's time to let go so Maverick/we can embrace what is new and ahead.

"Forget the former things; do not dwell on the past. See, I am doing a new thing! Now it springs up; do you not perceive it? I am making a way in the wilderness and streams in the wasteland."
Isaiah 43:18-19 NIV

Even in the church sometimes people want the old hymns, the old ways, the same old things that were done years ago but God says, "Sing to me a new song." There's something that he's doing for us in the new and He makes all things new. It's not that you can't love the old hymns, I have my favorites, but don't be resistant to the new, great worship songs being created.

So don't nail your foot to the floor of the past. It's time to let go! Don't keep yourself looping your mistakes, sins, or failures, don't hang on to shame, anger, or bitterness. Know that He's made you a new creation in Christ Jesus. The old is gone, behold the new has come! God has already let go of it for you it's time for you to let it go!

Years ago my daughter, husband and I were in a skit for a women's retreat. In this drama the daddy kept asking a little girl to give him her pearls. She didn't want to part with these dime-store, cheap pearls when he asked her for them. But he kept asking so that he could give her a strand of beautiful real ones. Yet she was reluctant. (*It's time to let go!*)

"Sweetie, will you give me your pearls?"
"No, Daddy not my pearls."

Unless she gave up the old cheaply made ones she could not receive the real, extremely valuable strand of pearls he intended to give her instead. But he didn't tell her about the exchange, he just needed her to trust his love and kept asking.

It's time to let go!

What do you need to let go of? Ask Holy Spirit to reveal it to you. When the revelation comes be quick to let it go. So you can embrace the good things that are ahead for you. Every good and perfect gift is from the Father so maybe it is time to let go to receive.

WHO I AM IN CHRIST

I AM GOD'S

TEMPLE & POSSESSION (1 Cor. 6:19-20)
CHILD (John 1:12)
WORKMANSHIP (Eph. 2:10)
FRIEND (John 15:15)
CHOSEN (Eph. 1:4)

I AM

COMPLETE IN HIM (Col. 2:10)
FREE FROM SIN'S POWER (Rom. 6:14)
SANCTIFIED (1 Cor. 6:11)
LOVED (1 John 4:9-10, 19)
LOVED FOREVER (Rom. 8:35-39)
KEPT BY GOD'S POWER (1 Peter 1:5)
NOT CONDEMNED (Rom. 8:1-2)
SEATED IN HEAVEN WITH CHRIST (Eph. 2:6)
A CITIZEN OF HEAVEN (Phil. 3:20)
HIDDEN WITH CHRIST IN GOD (Col. 3:3)
SECURE IN CHRIST (John 10:28-29)
MORE THAN A CONQUEROR (Rom. 8:37)

I HAVE BEEN

WASHED IN THE BLOOD OF THE LAMB (Rev. 1:5)
REDEEMED BY HIS BLOOD (1 Peter 1:18-19)
SET FREE FROM SIN (Rom. 8:2)
SET FREE FROM DARKNESS (Col. 1:13)
CHOSEN BEFORE TIME (Eph. 1:4)
PREDESTINED TO BE LIKE JESUS (Rom. 8:29)
FORGIVEN OF ALL MY SINS (Col. 2:13-14)
ADOPTED AS AN HEIR (Rom. 8:15-17)

I HAVE BEEN GIVEN

AN ETERNAL INHERITANCE (1 Peter 1:5)
A SOUND MIND (2 Tim. 1:7)
A HOME IN HEAVEN (John 14:1-6)
THE HOLY SPIRIT (2 Cor. 1:22)
ALL THINGS FOR LIFE (2 Pet. 1:3)
INCREDIBLE PROMISES (2 Pet. 1:4)
ACCESS TO GOD (Eph. 3:12)

BOOKMARK
This was used at a retreat and I was given the rights to share it with my audiences and here with you.

Say these aloud and declare them over yourself as the truths that need to **REPLACE** any of the nonsense lies that come your way. Declare them loudly and with conviction. Scripture says *out of your belly rivers of living water will flow.* So I want you to say this out loud as you read them and declare them over yourself. Say them like you own them and like you mean them. And by the way, Jesus bought these for you to be able to declare. So don't hold back. Even if you're an introvert, within your introvertedness, give me everything you've got! I am not robbing you of your personality but within your personality, give me everything you've got. Are you ready?

Here are some key passages that will help solidify your identity in Christ. As you awaken to who you truly are, use Scripture to cement that. Fill your mind with God's word and what he says about you. If you want this book to bring transformation, ask Holy Spirit to make these passages and verses come alive and bring revelation to you. You'll never be the same it's a game changer.

Key passages:

Romans 5:12-21
1 John 5:18
2 Peter 1:3
Ephesians 1: 1-14
Ephesians 2:1-10
Colossians 1:9-14
2 Corinthians 5: 6-21
2 Corinthians 1: 19-22.
Deuteronomy 14:2
Galatians 3:29

Is your identity in crisis or in Christ?
Whose view do I have of myself?
Whose voice am I listening to?
When the world is asking, "Who am I?" We can respond, "I know who I am in Christ."

Declare these aloud:
I am who God says I am! So I know who I am!
- I am loved. John 15:9; Romans 8:38-39
- I am adequate in Christ. 2 Corinthians 3:5-6
- I have the Spirit's power. Acts 1:8; Ephesians 1:19
- God rejoices over me. Zephaniah 3:17; Isaiah 62: 5b
- I am significant. Psalm 139:1-16
- I can approach the throne boldly. Hebrews 4:16
- I am able to pull down strongholds. 2 Corinthians 10:3-5
- I have everything I need for life and godliness. 2 Peter 1:3

After you've read through this and declared them over yourself shout, "Hallelujah!"

Here's a thought. Physical demonstration can bring about spiritual release so, I have an idea. How about you put your hands out in front of you, as a prophetic gesture of faith that you will be receiving something as I pray for you? Hands out, palms up like you're gladly receiving a wonderful package. Here's my prayer for you:

Father, thank you so much for the truths of these things because you bought them. Thank you for who you are. Thank you God that our identity can be secure instead of in crisis. We can have our identity in Christ.

Lord, we don't need to run around trying to please you, you have already performed perfectly through the blood of Christ on our behalf. So we don't have to perform to receive or earn your love. Thank you God.

I thank you for this beloved reader. I thank you that these truths will be not only foundational but expounded on through this book. I thank you that you've designed and desired to put truth into our hearts. Sow what is already seeds of truth, I ask you to water them and make them grow. And I thank you Holy Spirit, I thank you Jesus Christ and we love you God the father. In the name of Jesus, Amen.

Chapter 9
Silver ID Bracelet

Believers, those of you who know Christ, did you know that the Bible in 1Peter chapter 2 calls you a Royal Priest?
And in Romans calls you co-heirs with Christ? A child of the King of kings is who you are.
In Ephesians, it says you are God's masterpiece, his poem his workmanship.
In 1 John 4:17 it says, as he is so are we now in this world.
This is who you are. So let's settle who we are and whose we are.

Let me ask you a few questions:
- What would it look like if you actually believed God's word about yourself?
- Do you view yourself this way?
- How would you treat yourself and others if you really knew that you walked in favor and were loved by the King of Kings?
- What would the generosity in your life look like if you believed your father owned the cattle on a thousand hills and had more than enough to provide for your every need?
- What would your thought life be like if you knew that you were completely loved and accepted by the king?

Take a moment, close your eyes, if you're willing and ask God for deeper revelation of your identity as a masterpiece and a royal daughter/son of the King of Kings.

As we think about who we are in Christ, our identity becomes secure in him. It's really important we know that we know for certain who we are. I'm praying even this book will be a tool that will cause an awakening to who you really are.

I told you about the tooth fairy and my son's drama regarding losing the tooth in our neighbor's sandbox. For some reason I kept all of my children's baby teeth. Do you know anybody else or have you ever done that?

One day I was looking for something in my drawer and I came across an ID bracelet that was silver along with all those little tiny teeth. When I found it I thought, *Oh my goodness that's the identity bracelet I wore probably in grade school!*

The great thing about my wrist is it really never changed that much. So the ID bracelet still fit me! I mention it because in tiny print it says:

- Rachel Heggen, that was my maiden name.
- Then it shows my parent's address in Iowa, where I grew up.
- The next line had their home phone number. Until recently they still had a wall phone.
- Here's the deal, below all those pieces of information about my identity is written my father's name. My name is etched or engraved at the top but what's foundational is my father's name is at the bottom. It says, my Dad's name Richard.

Do you know what your Spiritual ID bracelet says? Do you know, the King of kings, God Almighty, is your father and your identity is secure in him? Your address is heaven and we are Citizens of Heaven just passing through here. And the phone number is important because my phone number listed on my ID bracelet is the phone number to my father.

You can always reach God. I call this His phone number: Jeremiah 33:3. It says, "*Call me and I will answer you and tell you great and mighty things that you don't already know.*" Man, I would raise my hand first. Raise your hand if you have anything in your life, a circumstance or situation that falls under this category, *you don't already know*? I am sure most of us would raise our hands and say, "I don't know everything."

So you've got a call to Him. I often say, "You gotta go to the throne, before you go to the phone." Too often we will call somebody or chat with a friend, a neighbor, our mentor, or mom. But let me remind you go to the throne before you go to the phone. Because God has already promised that He will answer you. He will tell you great and mighty things that you don't already know. Hallelujah!

I think it's really important that you understand what Scripture says about you. That is why I've been stressing it. We're going to turn a corner in a minute, I want to list some things from Ephesians, some of the core things that have formed my thoughts, convictions, and beliefs on identity come from Ephesians chapter 1 and chapter 2. Some of it comes from Colossians and other places in the Bible as well. And as I list these, I want you to know that it's important to know who you are and it comes from what God says about you in His word.

Oh, I love this quote I heard Bill Johnson say once in a sermon. He said, **"I can't afford to have a thought in my head about me that God doesn't have in his head about me."** Why don't you reread that quote. It's super powerful and true. Our view of who we are must completely line up with what God says about us. His word is the authority!

Chapter 10
Made on Purpose for a Purpose

I scooted out to my car, *oh, good it's only sprinkling. You lead tonight's study so you need to be on time.* I drove to church at dusk I thought, *it's going to be good to see each other, a nice night of Bible Study.* Little did I know, it would be a night my passions would be both fueled and satiated.

Passions? What am I passionate about you may be wondering? Break-through, in any form. I love to help break down barriers that impede the path to God. I get a fire in my belly and a rise in my spirit when there's an opportunity to tear down what prevents us from seeing God or ourselves clearly. It is part of my identity in Jesus.

This is my goal too and I relate to these verses in Colossians 1:28, 29 from The Passion Translation: *Christ is our message! We preach to awaken hearts and bring every person into the full understanding of truth. It has become my inspiration and passion in ministry to labor with a tireless intensity, with his power flowing through me, to present to every believer the revelation of being his perfect one in Jesus Christ*.

When a person steps into who God has made them to be, they become transformed and unleashed. Once they embrace their significance it helps unlock the door to their mission and their life's purpose becomes clearer. It's so exciting!

I believe, WE WERE MADE ON PURPOSE FOR A PURPOSE! Take a moment to say aloud, "I am made on purpose for a purpose."

Back to the Bible Study. We caught up a bit then recited our memory verse.

For we are God's handiwork, created in Christ Jesus to do good works which God prepared in advance for us to do. Ephesians 2:10

One translation reads: WORKMANSHIP = POEM.

Stop and let that truth sink in. You are God's poem. His beautiful, hand-written poem. He is the master creator. You are His masterpiece and he doesn't make junk. He wants you to be you! He has prepared in advance the things you are to do.

Here's a way I think about God's preparation in life. Long ago when our kids were small, if I asked my husband to give our child or the new baby a bath he'd willingly do it. He was very helpful, still is.

Here's the thing, prior to requesting his help I had:

- Run the bath water

- Set out the baby shampoo

- gathered the towel

- laid out the new diaper and PJ's

- grabbed the small hairbrush and body lotion

THE BATH EXPERIENCE WAS ALL SET UP AND READY TO GO! I had prepared in advance the things my husband was to do. Namely, give the baby a bath.

Basically ALL he had to do was simply wash him off! I had prepared everything in advance for the task of bathing the baby. Honestly, there were times when I'd think… *I may as well have given the kid the bath myself.*

It's a very simplistic story, I know, but it illustrates how God prepares in advance what we are to do. He made us so He knows what we are hard-wired to do. You are his handiwork/poem and He has things prepared and He is good. So I implore you, don't get your undies in a bunch and trust Him.

There is a Divine mystery - a secret surprise that has been concealed from the world for generations but now it's being revealed, unfolded and manifested for the holy believer to experience. ***Living within you is the Christ,*** *who floods you with the expectation of glory!* ***This mystery of Christ, embedded within us,*** *becomes a heavenly treasure chest of hope filled with the riches of glory for his people and God wants everyone to know it.* Colossians 1 :26-28 TPT Emphasis mine.

Back to the night of my Bible study…

It seemed to become holy ground for me. As women chimed in, we helped each other see the way God has formed us, it was beautiful to witness. We read from 1 Corinthians 12 about the body and how we are not the same. We are different parts of the body with different gifts, all with the same Spirit.

One of the reasons I am on the planet is to help people celebrate their significance and the genius of God in them, so as you might imagine, I was so pumped about the way our evening related to purpose and mission.

So let me ask you. What is your purpose or mission? What are you SHAPED to do? How have you been shaped by God? This "SHAPE" concept is not mine, but it's one of the chapters of Rick Warren's book, The Purpose Driven Life. Perhaps you've read it. Do you know your shape?

S - Spiritual Gifts - to each is given the manifestation of the spirit for the common good. The utterance of wisdom, knowledge, faith, gifts of healing, working in miracles, prophecy, distinguishing between spirits, tongues, interpretation. To touch on a few from First Corinthians chapter 12.

H - Heart - What do you care about? To whom are you compassionate?

A - Abilities - What are you good at and enjoy doing?

P - Personality - How has God wired you?

E - Experiences - Things you have encountered and done are different than other individual's collection of experiences. Don't discount or dismiss anything.

Think about your SHAPE. **You have been shaped, by God, on purpose for a purpose.**

SHAPE: Jot some things down in the space below, if you'd like.

Whether you are an introvert or extrovert, whether you play an instrument or make spreadsheets, whether you have the gift of wisdom, teaching, or hospitality, all of your days and painful experiences help define your purpose. You are shaped on purpose for a purpose.

There never has been anyone on this planet like you and there never will be again. You are uniquely created by God. You are His poem, His masterpiece! The way you are shaped helps define more clearly your purpose and mission.

Since I love to help people celebrate their significance and the genius of God in them, I was LIT UP and thrilled that night. I was among world changers! Check out who was seated with me:

- A comedian and compassionate helper of the weak
- A sold out university student resolved to follow Christ and call her generation to holiness and to be the best version of herself
- A nurse who wears, like Jesus, "the towel" of a servant with style
- A wise teacher who ignites people's hunger for God's word as they learn to feed on the word of God themselves
- A woman sent by the Holy Spirit to the masses
- A children's author called to implore others to "cease striving" and rest in God's faithfulness

A key memory verse. Ephesians 2:10 *For we are God's handiwork, created in Christ Jesus to do good works which God prepared in advance for us to do.*

We're NOT all alike! That's the beauty of the way God designed the body. Know this! So go out **boldly** in your SHAPE, living your life on purpose! Please know, I celebrate your significance and the genius of God in you. Beloved, arise, shine!

Scripture for your consideration:

I Corinthians 12:4-27 *There are different kinds of spiritual gifts, but the same Spirit is the source of them all. There are different kinds of service, but we serve the same Lord. God works in different ways, but it is the same God who does the work in all of us. A spiritual gift is given to each of us so we can help each other. To one person the Spirit gives the ability to give wise advice; to another the same Spirit gives a message of special knowledge. The same Spirit gives great faith to another, and to someone else the one Spirit gives the gift of healing. He gives one person the power to perform miracles, and another the ability to prophesy. He gives someone else the ability to discern whether a message is from the Spirit of God or from another spirit. Still another person is given the ability to speak in unknown languages, while another is given the ability to interpret what is being said. It is the one and only Spirit who distributes all these gifts.* ***He alone decides which gift each person should receive.***

One Body with Many Parts

The human body has many parts, but the many parts make up one whole body. So it is with the body of Christ. Some of us are Jews, some are Gentiles, some are slaves, and some are free. But we have all been baptized into one body by one Spirit, and we all share the same Spirit. Yes, the body has many different parts, not just one part. If the foot says, "I am not a part of the body because I am not a hand," that does not make it any less a part of the body? And if the ear says, "I am not part of the body because I am not an eye," would that make it any less a part of the body? If the whole body were an eye, how would you hear? Or if your whole body were an ear, how would you smell anything?

But our bodies have many parts, and God has put each part just where he wants it. How strange a body would be if it had only one part!

Yes, there are many parts, but only one body.

The eye can never say to the hand, "I don't need you." The head can't say to the feet, "I don't need you."

In fact, some parts of the body that seem weakest and least important are actually the most necessary. And the parts we regard as less honorable are those we clothe with the greatest care. So we carefully protect those parts that should not be seen, while the more honorable parts do not require this special care. So God has put the body together such that extra honor and care are given to those parts that have less dignity.

This makes for harmony among the members, so that all the members care for each other. If one part suffers, all the parts suffer with it, and if one part is honored, all the parts are glad. ***All of you together are Christ's body and each of you is a part of it.*** Emphasis mine.

He uses it all and nothing is wasted!

Chapter 11
Words Create Worlds

Let me illustrate something for you. Pretend you have someone, a friend of yours, standing in front of you. Can you picture them? Okay, now I'm going to begin to talk to them the way some of you talk to yourself. I'm going to begin to say the kind of things you hear - the voices inside your own head. You may speak internally over yourself, without even realizing it.

WATCH OUT! There is a progression of sorts. First you hear the voice, then you partner with what you've heard. Maybe even when it's a lie, you agreed with the lie and you believed it. WARNING: If you haven't *recognized, rejected and renounced and replaced* the lie, it can be detrimental.

As Bill Johnson says, *when you believe a lie you empower the liar!* You see the lie itself has no power, it's simply nothing, it would fall flat on the floor with no effect but it's when we believe a lie, partner with it, attach ourselves to it, come into agreement with it or adopt it, that's when we empower the liar.

When you are listening to negative voices, you may say these types of things over yourself. Back to my illustration. Just think if I had a dear friend of yours standing right in front of you and I began speaking to them this way, "You know what? You're stupid. You can't get it together. Your future is not bright! You know you should not have done that. What were you thinking? You're pathetic! Oh, and what you are going through, it's never going to change! You are so dumb and you've been dumb since fourth grade."

Aren't you uncomfortable as you read this? Even thinking about me saying these things to someone makes me very uneasy. I am such an encourager and encouraging words person I am uncomfortable typing them even now. Because they're not true! But some of you have no problem talking to yourself that way. Am I right?

You have **no problem** at all talking to yourself in a manner that is unhealthy and negative. And you've got a **stop it**! Because the truth is you're a masterpiece. God says your future is bright. He's got a future and a hope for you. You are well able and capable in Christ. Whatever you were able to do God is going to equip you to do it even better - exceedingly abundantly far beyond all you could ask or imagine! Those are the plans he has for you.

You get to go do what you do with complete confidence. So whatever I have said in this illustration even though it's a fictitious person that I was speaking over, I break that off now in the name of Jesus! I rebuke all of those slimy, negative and lying words off and I command them to go now, in the name of Jesus!

If I had a friend in front of me and I started speaking to her this way, wouldn't you think, *that's so rude, what are you doing?* Maybe you would even want to defend her. Or stop me from talking to her like that. I sure hope you would. Be careful of how you speak to yourself!

This situation really happened to me a few years back. I was making some food for a friend's, daughter's wedding. I wanted to go over and help, be a worker-bee. *What do you need? How can I help you?* We decided to make some pasta salad for the reception. I was there to do anything really, whatever she needed.

We both stood in her kitchen at the island and worked together but it wasn't long before she started to say things to herself out loud. I heard her because I stood there working directly beside her. She mocked, "You can't figure this out. What's wrong with you? Oh, brother, you forgot things outside. You're so blah, blah, blah," she rattled on even a bit under her breath at one point.

Then, I interrupted, "Hey, you are so good to me. You're such a good friend. Could you just stop? Please be as nice to yourself as you are to me!"

She briefly walked out of the sliding glass door, stepped onto the back deck and grabbed a few tomatoes ripening outside on a patio hightop table. As she came back inside, she quickly closed the screen door, scrunched up her face, looked directly at me and admitted, "Oooh, I do that, don't I?"

Let me ask you, how do you speak to yourself? Do you talk badly, speak in an unkind or derogatory manner? You may not even be aware you are doing it. Or perhaps you know full well you do it and are so used to it. Do you listen to the negative voices or have you become the negative voice yourself?

Maybe you don't even know you've partnered with the lies or negativity, because it's never been exposed. *Well, maybe I do, but I'd never let it come out of my mouth!* My example may seem extreme, but it's no better, nor less damaging, if you just let it ping around in your head. You see, it leaves the same wreckage. Either way it's NOT okay! Maybe you'd like to repent right now and think on a higher level. Ask God to forgive you for the way you have spoken to, of, and about His creation, you. Ask Holy Spirit to give you his thoughts about how he sees you.

I heard a quote once "Be kind to yourself, you're the only 'you' you've got!" The truth is, you must agree with what God says about you and He has plenty to say in the Word. Rejoice and relax. You get to be you. He made you; you are a masterpiece! Stop beating yourself up and allow the Word to build you up.

Chapter 12
The Real Deal

My father passed a few years ago. Golly, I miss him like CRAZY! He was a clever man, an inventor of sorts, a masterful artist, a mentor to many, an incredible storyteller, a wonderful Spirit-filled human and definitely a hero in my life. He was the real deal!

A few years before his passed away, I started a podcast and he was the inspiration and reason for the title. By the way, those of you who are podcast listeners, I'm sure you would enjoy it and I'd love for you to subscribe, it's called "the real deal." Real people, real stories and a real God. My purpose is stated in the tag line... Rachel Inouye - Helping people celebrate their significance and the genius of God in them.

My dad was RD, Richard Dean and he always told us *just be the R.D., the real deal.* It was wonderful advice. If you're a parent or grandparent just tell your children and grandchildren be the real deal. *Be authentically you.* For example, If you don't like to hike or run around out in the woods because you don't like the outdoors, it's OK. If you love the outdoors and everybody in your family sits inside and lays on the couch all the time it's OK. Be who you are!

My dad blessed me to be the real deal. I named the podcast, "the real deal" and he was my first guest and the episode aired on his 87th birthday. I've actually interviewed so many incredible people, each one comfortable in their own skin. They like being who they are and that's why I wanted to interview them. They're the real deal.

When it comes to your identity you need to be who God crafted and designed you to be. He is pleased with His work.You are free to be you. My father was the real deal and it helped shape me even as a young girl. His influence left a profound impact on me. He led mainly by example. Dad was comfortable in his own skin, he liked being Richard and not only that, he always encouraged me to be me.

Now, if that's true in the natural, with an earthly father, think of how true it is in the spiritual realm. God says, *Listen, I wired you, I made you, I've given you a personality and I've given you certain places to live.* In Acts chapter 17 it says, "He designs the exact time and places in which we live." Even if we think it's by accident or our own choice, God says. "*No, that's where you're gonna live. And those are the people you're gonna hang out with, and that's the church you're gonna go to and those are the people you'll work with.*"

You may say, "God I don't really like those people at my job!"

And God says, "*I know, that's why I have you there.*"

So it's really important that you know who you are and whose you are and come into alignment with what God has said about you. He knows you. Consider Psalm 139. "…He knows when you sit and when you rise; He is familiar with all your ways. Before a word is on your tongue, He knows it completely…" There isn't anywhere you can go that is beyond His gaze or distant from His presence.

We have to get passed any separation mindset. God is near, close, inside of the believer. We are one, we have union with Him. God put us in Christ and Christ in us. I hear Graham Cooke ask, "How can you get away from the one you contain? Part of your identity is to accept this union with Emanuel, God with us."

I think it is Bobby Connor who said, "Heaven and Hell are both asking, **'Who do you think you are?'"**

It is so vital that you know who you are IN CHRIST and whose you are. You are a child of the Most High God and you are blessed, forgiven, accepted, chosen, dearly loved. I just get so excited for truth to be embraced. I desire for all people to **get off the porch**, **break out of the box** of their own limiting thoughts or beliefs which they've kept themselves or God in. I long to see the son's of God **leave the pew** and be released to the watching world. **Arise and Shine!**

I want you to read from Ephesians. I want your ears to perk up, so read it aloud if you're able. You'll find you will say many things from the Scriptures that are true about you. Receive it! Take it in, it's all what God has said about you. Some of us are trying so hard to perform so we can be loved by God when there's no performance necessary. Wow! So much has been won for you. The finished work of Jesus Christ is amazing! What he performed was a done deal. It's incredible the things that have been won for us. We get to believe and receive.

Ephesians 1: 1-14 *"Paul, an apostle of Christ Jesus by the will of God, To the saints who are in Ephesus, and are faithful in Christ Jesus: Grace to you and peace from God our Father and the Lord Jesus Christ. Blessed be the God and Father of our Lord Jesus Christ, who has blessed us in Christ with every spiritual blessing in the heavenly places, even as he chose us in him before the foundation of the world, that we should be holy and blameless before him. In love he predestined us for adoption to himself as sons through Jesus Christ, according to the purpose of his will, to the praise of his glorious grace, with which he has blessed us in the Beloved. In him we have redemption through his blood, the forgiveness of our trespasses, according to the riches of his grace, which he lavished upon us, in all wisdom and insight making known to us the mystery of his will, according to his purpose, which he set forth in Christ as a plan for the fullness of time, to unite all things in him, things in heaven and things on earth.*

In him we have obtained an inheritance, having been predestined according to the purpose of him who works all things according to the counsel of his will, so that we who were the first to hope in Christ might be to the praise of his glory. In him you also, when you heard the word of truth, the gospel of your salvation, and believed in him, were sealed with the promised Holy Spirit, who is the guarantee of our inheritance until we acquire possession of it, to the praise of his glory."

What I want for you to know and observe, even though you have only read the first fourteen verses, we've not even completed the whole first chapter of Ephesians, but it repeats "**in him"** and tells you that **you are a saint.**

Declare these aloud with boldness:
- I am a saint!
- I receive grace
- I have peace
- I am chosen
- I am holy
- I am adopted
- I am blessed
- I am redeemed
- I am forgiven of sin
- I am predestined
- I am sealed

I haven't made any of that up. This was straight from the first part of Ephesians. May I suggest an activation or exercise? Just sit down with a pad of paper and write these down when you open your Bible. As you read them aloud jot him down. So far we've only covered a few, just a few and they were right there in the first chapter of Ephesians.

You know what? When you feel you are not selected and God doesn't have you on his team, no no no, you refute it with I'm chosen! Or you hear *Oh, boy, you've really messed up,* you can say *no no no I'm forgiven!* Do you understand? You have to agree with God and what God says about you. Those lies will keep you on the porch and in the box but that's not where you belong beloved.

Chapter 13
Where Are You?

I've asked you previously these questions:
- Who are you?
- Whose are you?
- Whose view do you have of yourself?
- Whose voice are you listening to?

Now I have another question for you… **Where are you?** That's a question God asked Adam in Genesis. It's an important question for us as well because it deals with our identity. We are new creations, created in Christ Jesus and where we are is important too.

I'd like you to read from chapter 2 of Ephesians just a few verses, but Chapter 2's words are very important as well! Starting with Ephesians 2:6 *"and raised us up with him and seated us with him* ***in the heavenly places*** *in Christ Jesus,"* Emphasis mine.

You have an aerial view of the world. You are seated with Christ in heavenly places, plural. The enemy wants to you to think you are only on the world in the natural realm. And that he is after you and you are running away. I can't tell you how many times I hear people say, "The enemy is after me and he's winning!" or "he's overtaking me!"

No, no, no! The enemy is not overtaking you, you are seated in the heavenly realm with Christ. So you have to take your spot! Because, guess what? You are above him and get to crush his head. Does that make sense?

The enemy is running after you? No, no, no, he's running away from you. You're a threat! You're seated, with Christ, in heavenly places. Where'd you get that? It's in the book, the Bible, right in Ephesians.

"...and raised us up with him and ***seated us with him in the heavenly places*** *in Christ Jesus, so that in the coming ages he might show the immeasurable riches of his grace in kindness toward us in Christ Jesus.*

Ephesians 2:8-10: *"For by grace you have been saved through faith. And this is not your own doing; it is the gift of God,"*

this is not of your own doing, (thank goodness!)

It is the gift of God – not by works, so that no one can boast. For we are God's handiwork, created in Christ Jesus to do good works which God prepared in advance for us to do. Emphasis mine.

Remember how many times it says, "to the praise of his glory." You are God's grand design! His glory on display. His grand ta-da!

I heard a speaker say that once and I will never forget it. I owned it. "I am God's ta-da!"

Say it aloud and say it proud. "I am God's ta-da!" I love to watch gymnastics especially during the Olympics. I gobble up the stories and the backgrounds of the young competitors. I delight to watch those girls go flip, flip, flip, flip, in the floor exercise competition and the bars and balance beam, but the floor exercise routines are my favorite part of the competition. Those young girls are so petite and they do their dismount or final pose where their back is completely swayed and they look like a banana with their arms completely in the air and posed. When they finish, I don't care if they've messed up or stumbled in the routine at some point, they still end this way. It's a stick-the-landing thing. And when they do I think, "TA-DA!"

Well, imagine that you are God's grand pose, his ta-da! That's what you are. You are God's masterpiece! It doesn't matter that you made mistakes. It doesn't matter if you don't feel like you measure up because He has ALREADY done it all and he just wants you to receive that. It's very freeing!

I told you earlier that my father was an artist and it's important to me. I'm grateful, because I have many things in my home that are his paintings and drawings. When people walk into my home they say, "Oh wow! That's great and wonderful. Did you do that?"

And I answer, "No, I did that one and that painting over there, but this one's my dad's work."

Now, I've NEVER had this happen, but if by way of illustration, anyone were to come in and were to look at my dad's paintings and say, "Whoa, that's just junk, who did that?"

Oh, I'm telling you, I'd have fire in my belly! I might have rave, "That is a solid, amazing, piece of artwork. But maybe you don't understand it." Because my dad did do abstract type paintings and artwork, "That, you see, is a masterpiece! Let me tell you why. My dad knows design. Look at that little piece up there that's red, see it? Well, that's counterbalanced over on the other side too, see it's also red. He would know the viewers eye is going to travel from here over to there. And he created multiple masterpieces, just like that one! So don't you dare call it junk!"

Right? I'm so serious, that's what I would say because he created masterpieces. But here's the deal, we need to know, beyond the shadow of a doubt, that we are God's masterpiece. And some people, I'm just gonna be honest, some people in the church get really nervous with this message, they get so concerned because they think I might be telling you something that won't keep you humble. But all I have to tell you is you must know it. I call it, **GOD-FIDENCE!**

And when you know who you are you hold your head up with your crown held high. What does it say in Ephesians? **All of what He gave us is to the praise of His glory.** Do you understand? It's for the praise of **His glory**! The world out there is looking for those people who know they aren't always broken. And the future isn't always bleak. And it's US! So we have to step up and let them know. We've got to arise and shine!

But we are so worried that if we step up and let them know, people somewhere, somehow is gonna think we are arrogant. No! It's **God-fidence**. False humility is killing the church. Because it's based on us still. Self-focused. And false humility is a form of pride. Because we're consumed with ourself always looking at ourself, thinking we are nothing and just weak worms of the earth. I hope you can feel my passion about you knowing who you are and what was bought for you. I'd like to include another section of Scripture, something from Colossians chapter 1. Then I'd also like to write a declaration over you.

Are you ready? You better be ready for this truth! Let it sink in, it packs a powerful punch. He took you from one place, pulled you out, and transferred you, and permanently set you in another place! Colossians 1:13 ESV: *He has delivered us from the dominion of darkness and transferred us to the kingdom of his beloved Son, in whom we have redemption, the forgiveness of sins.*

If you transfer money today from one bank account to another. It's no longer in the first account. You understand that, right? The bank teller will give you a statement and it won't show that it's there in the first account, because you've transferred it to a different one.

He has transferred you from the dominion of darkness into the kingdom of light! It's important that you know and operate from that place. That is so vital. It's all part of knowing WHERE you are. You were bought with blood. A high price! In Deuteronomy 14 it says what God says about his kids:

Deuteronomy 14:2 *For you are a people holy to the LORD your God, and the LORD has chosen you to be a people for his treasured possession, out of all the peoples who are on the face of the earth.*

Whoa! Let that sink in, you are God's chosen, treasured possession. That's a big deal! Many times people come and talk to me saying, "No, no that is talking about the Israelites, those are the Jews, those are his chosen people, those are the people chosen by God."

And I understand what they are thinking and I reply, let's go to Galatians 3:29 in the NIV it says*: If you belong to Christ, then you are Abraham's seed, and heirs according to the promise.*

You must understand that we have not been barging our way in, we have been grafted in. So own what you own and where you are. Wouldn't it be terrible if your house were falling apart and you had a great inheritance of a new mansion but you never thought to move into it? Do you see what I'm saying? God says use this inheritance I'm giving you. It's a game changer when you know what those things are.

God is saying, in Ephesians 2, I've purchased, through Jesus, so much for you: your salvation, forgiveness, a place seated in heavenly places with me. I've given you authority, you are my chosen ones. You are co-heirs with Christ. You are a royal priesthood, a holy nation people belonging to God. I have given you glorious riches in Christ Jesus. I've put so many things on layaway in your life you get to just receive them knowing fully who you are and stepping into all that I have won for you. You fight from victory not for victory.

Here's my hope and great expectation for you: to know who you are, whose you are and where you are. I've listed these things from Colossians and Ephesians so that you will know where you were and where you are now. You have been transferred, from the dominion or darkness into the kingdom of light and that settles it. You are a child of light with a Father of Light who loves you lavishly in a kingdom of light. That is who, whose and where you are.

How you think about yourself, believer, must line up with God's word. I've mentioned all of that to say this: He says you're beloved so just, Be Loved!

You have a new name, no longer Sinner, now Saint. You live in the new covenant, transferred from a dominion to a Kingdom. You have a new nature, the old one is gone. It's dead! AND the new has come.

2 Corinthians 5:17 ESV *Therefore, if anyone is in Christ, he is a new creation. The old has passed away; behold, the new has come.*

Chapter 14
Mirror Mirror

There is a great deal more to be said about this topic than the cursory layout given in this chapter but since I believe it relates to identity let me briefly say:

It's simple to take the road easily traveled by the world and remain in the natural realm when it comes to certain aspects of our identity, like our appearance and our bodies. I speak most often to women, although I've had mixed audiences and I've addressed youth too. So I'd like to address women here and remind you, beloved, of who you are and help set this truth firmly in your identity.

- You ARE a spirit
- You HAVE a soul
- You LIVE in a body

Let me reiterate, you are SPIRIT that's your true identity. You are awakening to this truth. Praise God.

You are a spirit - wisdom, communion, conscience
You have a soul - mind, will and emotions
You live in a body - flesh, bone, blood

However, we can get so consumed by our bodies and a skewed body image results. This can lead to a downward spiral into self-consciousness, anxiety and attack on self-esteem where we curse our own bodies rather than care for and bless them.
Wait! Shouldn't we take care of our bodies? You may be wondering. Yes, absolutely! It's God's temple. We are His mobile home. The Holy Spirit indwells the believer. Jesus came to give

life and life to the full. We do need to bless our bodies and ask God how to take care of them so we can live to our optimal capacity and full purpose.

We are exhorted, in Scripture, *not to conform to the patterns of this world but be transformed by the renewing of our minds.* I often say, "mind your mind." So I'd ask again, "What are you thinking about? Whose view do you have of yourself?"

The world is obsessed with looks and appearances.

"Do not look on his appearance or the height of stature, because I have rejected him. For the LORD sees not as man sees: man looks on the outward appearance but the LORD looks on the heart." 1 Samuel 16:7

Charm is deceptive, and beauty is fleeting; but a woman who fears the LORD is to be praised. Proverbs 31:30

Yet our spirit is alive in Christ and needs feeding too.

It's tempting to allow the "mirror, mirror on the wall" to inform us of who we are but we must make the needed shift to "mirror, mirror of the Word" and let it form, transform, define and solidify our true identity.

Let me suggest you say this aloud and declare it: "I am who God says I am."

So repent of comparing yourself to other's bodies or even to a past version of your own self. Agree with God that you are fearfully and wonderfully made. Even if you'd like to make changes or get more healthy you can still turn down the emphasis placed on the body and feed your soul and spirit until the Spirit directs the soul and body to come into alignment too.

Chapter 15
Blood-Bought Child

You are the righteousness of God in Christ Jesus! What happened to the old nature? OK, remember how I mentioned earlier my grandmother passed away when I was a young mother. She lived an active and long life, just shy of 99 years.

But when she passed away, I no longer visited her. And she no longer visited me. Because she had passed away. That's a euphemism that means she died. She's dead. And because she had passed away she was no longer able to come visit me. Or be a force in my life. We must be careful not to think our old nature which has been crucified with Christ is still alive and has influence on us. It says, I no longer live but Christ lives in me! I am dead to sin and alive to righteousness.

Believer, blood-bought child of God, this is vital for your identity to be established and secure. Stop thinking you are a sinner. **Jesus was numbered with the transgressors, so you would never be!** I call it the GRAND SWAP! Think of what is yours given on His authority.

Read the chorus lyrics from Bill Gaither's song, "On His Authority."

On the authority of the Holy Word
I rise up and take my stand
I'm a blood bought child of the living God
Who is the Great I Am
I'm a heir to all the heaven holds
And no principality
Can ever take away my royal crown
Given on His authority

In the devotional, Morning and Evening, by Charles Spurgeon, this verse is mentioned in Morning March 30.
He poured out his soul to death and was numbered with the transgressors.
Isaiah 53:12

Let me include a portion of it here: "Our Lord Jesus was numbered with the transgressors in order that they might *feel their hearts drawn toward him.* Who can be afraid of the one who's name appears on the same list with us? Surely we may come boldly to him and confess our guilt. He who is numbered with us cannot condemn us. Was He not entered in the transgressors list *that we might be written in the red roll of the saints?* He was holy and written among the holy; we were guilty and numbered among the guilty. **He transfers his name from that list to this dark indictment, and our names are taken from the indictment and written in the roll of acceptance, for there is a complete transfer made between Jesus and His people.** All our conditions of misery and sin Jesus has taken; and all that Jesus has comes to us. His righteousness, His blood, and everything that He has he gives us as our dowry. Rejoice, believer, in your union to him who was numbered among the transgressors; and prove that you are truly saved by being clearly identified with those who are new creatures in Him." emphasis mine

Get this straight. Beloved, your old nature does not follow you. It is true that you had an old nature, but it does not follow you. It has passed away! You have a new nature. You are a new creation. You are a blood bought child and no longer have a sin nature. You may have a sin habit. But you are a saint. You are the righteousness of God in Christ Jesus. You are a holy one. You may have a sin habit but just as habits are formed, habits can be broken. The Holy Spirit is is given to give you power not to sin.

You have a kingdom GPS so when you go astray the GPS is recalculating, recalculating, recalculating! You are becoming more and more like Christ, that's sanctification. Don't dwell on the **past** think about your **position** that has been established. It is righteousness and it is in Christ. And that does not move.

You are more prone to righteousness than you are prone to sin. So when the enemy tries to tell you how dirty you are or accuses you and condemns you, remember, he is a liar! The battle between the good and the bad the old and the new is not a battle unless it's one in your own mind. You can win the battle of the mind by agreeing and believing God's word.

The Spirit of God has more power over you and we need to submit to him and the authority that he has in our lives. Who you are in Christ is more important than what you think about yourself or what the world will tell you. It is an established truth. Your identity is set in Christ. You are a royal priesthood a holy nation a person belonging to God. You are chosen, accepted, forgiven, adopted, royalty, victorious and an overcomer. Soak it up! Awaken to the truth of who you really are, it's a game changer.

So when false humility comes in and tries to tell you *you're a weak worm of the world. You're a sinful one.* And you think you can't hold your head up. That is not from God. You have God's DNA. You are God's mobile home. You are on the loose in the world. You are on display. He wants you to be out there! You get to shine! He is who you house. **Arise and shine!**

Jesus paid such a high price for us, too high for us to not fully claim and walk in the newness of life that he gave us. Does that make sense to you?

We exalt Jesus Christ when we claim what he has paid for. When we claim what he has purchased for us and walk in the identity and the newness of life he has given us. If it makes sense you say it aloud, **"I receive it."**

It's such good news! It's been paid for in full. And you can step into it. If you know Jesus you just need to say, "God, thank you, thank you, thank you, thank you, thank you, thank you, I'm so thankful, thank you God!"

I've heard the logic that if someone were to give me a compliment or give me praise that I should not accept it. Because that would rob God of his glory. Are you kidding me? Do you realize when you say thank you to God, and run to him and give him the glory you've never robbed him of the glory. In fact in John 17, Jesus says that the glory that was given him he gives to us. How can I be robbing him of something he gave to me? Let me mention here one verse:

John 17:22, 23 The glory that you have given me I have given to them that they may be one even as we are one, I in them and you and me, that they may become perfectly one, so that the world may know that you sent me and loved them even as you loved me.

Chapter 16
Ice Skater

Let me offer an illustration of giving glory to God, not robbing him of it. I had a friend call me to catch up and during our conversation she said, "My workplace had a party for me, a 'departing celebration' because I'm going to a new company. It was a farewell celebration where so many people approached me and told me things like, "You know, if you weren't here, I don't know what I would have done." "I don't know where my marriage would've been, if you weren't here, thanks for your support!" "I don't think I would've been able to stand it in this company so long if it weren't for you.""

Do you understand she was *re-presenting* God when she was there at her place of employment, right? Regarding the farewell celebration, I inquired, "How did you take that? Did you receive it? Did you accept it?"

And she responded hesitantly, "What are you talking about, Rachel what do you mean?"

I stated, "So many Christians cannot accept anything positive about themselves because they're worried if they accept the praise or complements it might cause them to turn into an egomaniac or at the least lack humility! I'm just curious, did you accept their sincere kudos and honor?"

She said, "Yes! Well, I think I did." I quickly mentioned how I had seen a picture when she told me about the party and how the people said, *I don't know where my marriage would have been; I don't know where my child would've been; I don't know if I could have stood working here this long, etc…* All I could think of was the picture I saw of an ice-skater. Yep! That's what my 'vision' or picture that formed so I told my friend about it and I'm telling you too. The thought/picture may have come to me because my daughter-in-love is an ice-skater, who knows.

In this picture I got, about how the skater finished their routine, they stand stationary in their final pose, meanwhile the members of the audience applaud, rise to their feet and toss roses or even bouquets on the ice.

They throw roses out onto the ice to signify their delight as if the roses each means, *wow, yay, way to go or that was brilliant!* And then, a volunteer enters the rink and collects all the roses then hands them to the competitor who just performed. Still breathing heavily from the routine, the cameras show the skater or couple as they sit and wait in the little box until their scores are announced.

Keep this in mind, whenever you receive a compliment, approval or accolades. It's all to the praise of HIS glory! So take the roses. Seriously, take the roses! Because this is what you get to do with them, you now give them away. It's a privilege and it does not rob God of His glory. You may hand the roses, *the compliments so to speak*, up to God. You now give him an offering of gratitude, "Here, God, thanks so much this is what they said about us." And you give the arm load of roses to Him, to the praise of His glory.

Do you understand? It is so humbling and freeing! Because the truth is, you are amazing, a masterpiece, a poem of God. And I am here to tell you or remind you today as you read this.
So, get your tights unstuck because when you collect your roses you get to say, "This is what I've got for you God. This is what they said about us! THANK YOU! You made me! And you formed me, and you've got a good plan for me, and you are going

out ahead of me. I know your Word says you prepare in advance the things I'm to do, so if I receive any accolades, you've already prepared them for me. So thanks!"

I implore you, would you please get it! Seriously! Would you please get it! It's part of your identity… You display His glory!

Arise, shine for your light has come, and the glory of the LORD has risen upon you. Isaiah 60:1

Chapter 17
Please Line Up!

I have a friend, SueAnn, who lives in the Twin Cities. I used to live there too. We prayed together when I lived near her and we were part of the same church. We prayed together for years on Thursdays. What I loved about praying with SueAnn is that if Thursday came and if we forgot to pray or didn't get a chance to pray together we always had Friday! She is a gift to me and so is prayer.

One time, I called her and said, "Let's pray today, does now work for you?" It was the start of the school year and at the time she was a preschool teacher. I had a little notebook that I would write down her prayer requests and praises of answered prayers. I also wrote mine and dated them.

I reminded her as we spoke on the phone, "I'm looking in my notebook and you said that you wanted prayer for the start of the school year with your little pre-schoolers, I'm just wondering how that's going? You said that you were going to be teaching them about the calendar, the seasons, and colors and things like that. How is that going? I have been praying for you."

And she said, "Rachel, we haven't gotten to the calendar! We haven't gotten to the seasons… We're still working on lining up!"

I laughed so hard because I pictured SueAnn with her students instructing them, "Okay, everybody lineup!" and the kindergarteners all go in different directions instead of forming a line. For her it would be like herding cats.

That's what I was thinking, so I asked, "So, what are you doing? How are you working on it?"
She replied, "Well, here's what I decided to do. We had already learned the colors so I decided to use colors to help them line up!" She continued, "for example I would say, 'If you're wearing blue, you can line up.' But they would all just sit there!"

She continued, "I decided to use a song to see if that would help." And she began to sing, '*If you are wearing blue, please line up!*'"

She had a long pause and then she blurted, "BUT they'd just sit there. Rachel, seriously, we're still working on lining up! Here's what I tried next, I started calling out individual names in the song, '*Wyatt you are wearing blue so you can line up! Brittany, you're wearing blue go ahead and line up. Timothy you're wearing BLUE YOU CAN line up!'* Rachel, I'm telling you, we are still working on LINING UP!"

I got to thinking about that. I'm effected by what I see and it teaches me a spiritual truth or a lesson. That was the catalyst for my first book, Lily Pads. Something in the natural realm speaks of the spirit realm. So I started thinking about lining up and then God gave me this thought.

I asked Him, "God what's the deal with lining up?"

And he said, "Well, think about it logically. They were not lining up so it could be they don't know their colors or they think that they need to be called out by name before they can line up."

So either they don't know their colors or they think they have to be called out individually. That's why!

I asked God, *what does that mean?* And this is what I believe He said. You need to know your colors! The believer, every man and woman, boy and girl each need to know their colors. God impressed this on me. *They need to know what I say about them, they need to know what I've purchased for them. They must know who they are in the kingdom. They've got to stop cooperating and partnering with lies and just step in…"*

So **"If you're wearing the blood, please line up!"** Do you get it?

Because if you're wearing the blood, all that it purchased applies to you! Do you get it? It's vital that you know your colors in the kingdom. What it says about you in the Word of God, beloved, is your true identity. The blood of Jesus covers and includes YOU. You don't have to be called out individually to line up for his promises, his plans, or his purposes. No, just take his word for it. LINE UP! It is imperative to know what's already been purchased for you because otherwise you will strive and struggle and become "works-based" instead of grace-based. *Thanks be to God for his indescribable gift!* 2 Corinthians 9:15 NIV

Lyrics from song Under the Blood by Marty J. Nystrom that relates:

O the blood of the Passover Lamb
Is applied to the door of my life
No power of darkness could ever withstand
The force of the blood sacrifice
Though Satan will bring accusations
I let him know right where I stand
For now there is no condemnation
I'm under the blood of the Lamb.

I'm under the blood of the Lamb
That covers the guilt of my past
By the mercy of God holy and righteous I stand
I'm under the blood of the Lamb
I'm safe and secure from the enemy's plan
No weapon formed against me will stand
I'm under the blood of the Lamb.

The more you awaken to the true identity of who you really are a blood-bought child of the living God, a new creation in Christ, the light of the world, a warrior in the kingdom and overcomer, the more you will continue in union with Jesus receiving all he purchased for you. The natural flow and outcome is simple, you will SHINE.

So beloved, blood-bought child of the living God, "Please line up!"

Chapter 18
Give Away What You Carry

I cannot give you five dollars unless I have five dollars. If I have five dollars with me then I can give it to you. I cannot give you peace but if I'm carrying peace from the Prince of Peace I can release peace to you. It's vital you know what you carry and who you are. You can't give away what you don't carry; but you can give away what you do carry, right?

A few years ago, I was speaking at a women's retreat and I had the meat of an apple stuck in my teeth. After the Friday session we had caramel apples, popcorn and other autumn treats in the special lodge as part of the night's activities. I could just feel the apple stuck in my teeth but I didn't have any floss with me. Oh, can you believe it? It was just a crime!

Anyway, because I didn't have floss the whole time I was bugged by it and I couldn't get my toothbrush to dislodge it. So, in front of the group the next morning, I told the ladies about my dilemma. Trust me, it did have something to do with my talk and the point I was making.

As soon as I told the audience about it, I'll never forget what happened next, a lady from the fourth row, stood up, came down the center aisle, walked toward the stage with her right arm extended straight out at me.

She said, "HERE!" Then she retracted her hand for a second, opened the container of floss and pulled out a long piece. The sound of the floss unwinding caught my attention. She cut the piece free and handed it to me. "Here you go!" She gave me part of her floss!

I remember thinking *I want to hug you tighter than you could ever think or imagine* because it was fabulous and I needed some dental floss so badly. But she couldn't give away floss unless she was carrying floss. Yes, that's a silly example to teach or illustrate this spiritual principle. You impart and give away what you carry. You must have it to give it.

When you carry the light of the world you dispel the darkness. Jesus said, "I am the light of the world." Then he turned to his disciples and told them, "You are the light of the world." You get to shine.

There are so many people, even believers, who are so afraid of the world, worried that the darkness will get on them so they shrink back and don't shine. It's my hunch it's because they don't know exactly who they are, whose they are, where they are nor what they carry.

Let me share this from a talk I heard from Graham Cooke:
"The biggest fight you'll ever face is always about your identity. That's why you have the Holy Spirit as your personal trainer to establish that identity at a really high level. So that you operate from that identity all the time."

Chapter 19
You Reflect the Beauty You Believe You Contain

I want include this story or allegory. Some of you may have read or heard the story of Johnny Lingo. This relates to who you are and how you've been purchased and what God did for you as well as the price he paid.

It's called: The Eight Cow Wife

Long ago, in a primitive culture, it was required that before they married, the young men had to bargain with the girl's father for her. The fathers of the village demanded payment for their daughters generally in the form of cows. Three cows could buy an above-average wife, and four or five cows a very beautiful wife!

Johnny, the brightest, strongest, and most handsome man in the village loved Sarita. Sarita most generously could have been described as being plain. She was not truly ugly, but neither attractive. She was shy. She was also older than most girls at the time of marriage.

The villagers loved to gossip about the bargaining price of a girl. Some said Johnny might offer two or three cows. Others said Sarita's father might take one cow since nobody else was interested in her.

Johnny went to meet with Sarita's father and offered eight cows for her.

Everyone was astonished. That was the highest price ever paid for a bride in their village! Soon, Johnny herded eight cows to his future father-in-law. The wedding was held the same evening.

Time passed, Sarita changed. Her eyes dazzled, and she moved and spoke with striking grace and poise. People who came to the village and had never seen Sarita before remarked that she was the region's most beautiful woman.

Much later, someone asked Johnny why he paid such a high price for her. Why offer eight cows when he could have had her as his wife for less? Did he make such an offer to make her happy?

"Yes, I wanted her to be happy, but I wanted more than that. The most important thing that changes a woman is how she thinks about herself. Sarita believed she was worth nothing. Now she knows she is worth more than any other woman in the village." Johnny concluded, "I loved Sarita and no other woman. And I wanted to marry her. But I also wanted an eight-cow wife."

From Winning in the Land of Giants, p. 43 (Youth Edition), by Dr. William Mitchell

You notice from this story Sarita started to act the way she was thinking; she started to behave based on her thoughts. That's all part of taking our thoughts captive and making them obedient to Christ.

It's why I stress:
Recognize
Reject
Repent
Renounce
Replace

I also realize that because we think such poor things about ourselves, we try, through behavior, to earn something. **We can't keep trying to reach for something we have already been given. We must stop trying to achieve something we already are.** But the truth is when we get truth planted firmly in our minds and hearts it affects our outward behavior. The order matters, it's not the other way around. We must think and believe correctly in order to behave correctly.

When you understand your worth you'll live up to it. The value that is placed on a person greatly affects the way they value themselves. Let me pause and ask you… Do you know how much value you have? God says, "You are mine!" You can declare aloud this truth: "I am valuable I am a blood-bought child of The Living God!"

Knowing that you were ransomed from the futile ways inherited from your forefathers, not with perishable things such as silver or gold, but with the ***precious blood of Christ****, like that of a lamb without blemish or spot. He was foreknown before the foundation of the world but was made manifest in the last times for the sake of you who through him are believers in God, who raised him from the dead and gave him glory, so that your faith and hope are in God.* 1 Peter 1:18-21 ESV. Emphasis mine.

Chapter 20
Thrifting

Let me tell you something personal about me, I like to thrift. I admit it because I really do enjoy the hunt and the thrill of the find. Don't get me wrong I think it's great to find little boutiques and shop in them too. I get it some people might not want to ever go into a thrift store. I think it may have to do with the thought that if something didn't cost a lot, it is cheap. What do we think when something is more expensive? We automatically believe it has great value. We just do. We think, *Oh is that a Coach bag? Is that a Louis Vuitton original?* We think this way. We place higher value on things that cost a great deal.

I remember once going to a Silpada jewelry party. Perhaps you have heard of it and know what Silpada is. Well, I had never been to a Silpada party before. That evening, I got all dolled up, chose a cross necklace to wear, grabbed my keys and headed out the door. I arrived safely at my friend's home.

As I entered, She greeted me warmly, "I'm so glad you came!" I scanned the home quickly to get a lay of the land since I had never been to her house before. She then introduced me to the ladies in attendance, "feel free to look around and shop; there's also food over here in the kitchen." She then dashed off to answer the door. *Wow! There are so many beautiful things here*, I thought. Immediately one gal came toward me and commented, "Oh, Rachel, that is such a beautiful cross!" She pointed to my neck, "I really love it! Is it Silpada?"

"No, it is not." I replied.

She complimented me again, "Well, it is so beautiful!"

I smiled and quickly said, "Thank you!"

She then followed me around to a different area where other tables were set up and she came up again, "Well is your cross Brighton? I love that Cross!"

To which I replied, "No, it's not Brighton." I kept making my way around to a different area in the room but she still followed me and insistently inquired, "Is it Lia Sophia?"

I said, "Nope."

She followed me like a little puppy dog, she was like my shadow and so persistent. So finally, I stopped dead in my tracks and said to her, "Here's the deal. I bought this cross at Walmart. I took it off a circular ring because it was originally a keychain. I ripped it off the little metal circle then put on a small silver adapter so I could hang it off this slide necklace. I am wearing a $2.95 silver and diamond cross that isn't Silpada, it's Walmart!"

Here's why I said it to her the way I did. I said it because immediately, I don't know what it is about women, but we easily divide into categories. With the information given some might turn up their nose and think, *Okay, she's just bizarre! Walmart, really?*

While another group might think, *Aw! You clever girl, that's great!*

If it were Brighton, if it were Silpada, if it were Lia Sophia then some might think more of me. However, since it was a simple keychain from WALMART, others may think less.

But I didn't care either way. Because things don't define me and I know who I am! But that's not the only point. When does it matter how much was paid? The higher the price may be related to its value and worth, right? And people understand that. **Listen dear reader, you are valuable and incredible! The most expensive price has been paid for you, the precious blood of Jesus Christ!** And it's been applied to the door of the heart's of believers. The price is very costly; yet it is free for all.

As I finish up this chapter let me pray for you. So why don't you place your hands out, palms up like you're receiving a gift and let me bless you with this prayer:

Father, I thank you for the gift of this reader. I thank you for what you did in your kingdom when you made her. Thank you for who she is, thank you that you know her each by name. The hairs on her head you've numbered and you know the number of her days.

Thank you for her beauty. Thank you for her royalty, thank you that she is a chosen, holy nation, a person belonging to you, God. Thank you that she is the beloved of God. I pray she would be loved. I give you all the glory, in the name of Jesus. Amen!

Chapter 21
Sinner or Saint

I had a thought, let's do a little activity…Grab a pen and I will ask you a question and I'd like you to respond. It won't take you long. So you answer this question and then I will answer it out of scripture. The question I have for you is, what makes a sinner, a sinner? Write down your answer now please. Ready? Go! Take a few minutes to write it down here:

The question: What makes a sinner, a sinner?
A great answer is from Scripture. Scripture talks about death in Adam and life in Christ. OK? Remember **death in Adam** and **life in Christ**. We will compare and contrast what happened as a result of Adam and "the second Adam," Jesus Christ!

Romans 5:12-19. *Therefore, just as* ***sin*** *came into the world through* ***one man****, and death through sin, and so death spread to all men because all sinned - for sin indeed was in the world before the law was given, but sin is not counted where there is no law. Yet death reigned from Adam to Moses,* *even over those whose sinning was not like the transgression of Adam, who was a type of the one who was to come.*

But the free gift is not like the trespass. For if many died through ***one man's trespass****, much more have the grace of God and the free gift by the grace of that one man Jesus Christ abounded for many. And the free gift is not like* ***the result of that one man's sin.*** *For the judgment following one trespass* ***brought condemnation****, but the free gift following many trespasses brought justification. For if, because of* ***one man's trespass, death reigned through that one man****, much more will those who receive the abundance of grace and the free gift of righteousness reign in life through the one man Jesus Christ.*

Therefore, as ***one trespass led to condemnation for all men****, so one act of righteousness leads to justification and life for all men. For as by the* ***one man's disobedience the many were made sinners****, so by the one man's obedience the many will be made righteous. Now the law came in to increase the trespass, but where sin increased, grace abounded all the more,* Emphasis mine.

So we can see, quite clearly here, that what makes a sinner a sinner, is Adam's sin. Now let me ask this question, what makes a righteous man righteous? Write your answer here:

Let me include the same scripture again Romans 5:12-19 so you can re-read and look for and compare what you wrote as your answer to the question: What make a righteous man righteous?

Therefore, just as sin came into the world through one man, and death through sin, and so death spread to all men because all sinned - for sin indeed was in the world before the law was given, but sin is not counted where there is no law. Yet death reigned from Adam to Moses, even over those whose sinning was not like the transgression of Adam, who was a type of the one who was to come.
But the free gift is not like the trespass*. For if many died through one man's trespass,* ***much more have the grace of God and the free gift by the grace of that one man Jesus Christ abounded for many.*** *And the free gift is not like the result of that one man's sin. For the judgment following one trespass brought condemnation,* ***but the free gift following many trespasses brought justification.*** *For if, because of one man's trespass, death reigned through that one man,* ***much more will those who receive the abundance of grace and the free gift of righteousness reign in life through the one man Jesus Christ.***
Therefore, as one trespass led to condemnation for all men, ***so one act of righteousness leads to justification and life for all men.***
For as by the one man's disobedience the many were made sinners, ***So the one man's obedience the many will be made righteous.***
Now the law came in to increase the trespass, but where sin increased, ***grace abounded all the more,*** Emphasis mine.

Thanks be to God! Through the one man's obedience we gain righteousness. It is a free gift. We have to get this into our heads because our thinking affects our belief and our belief affects our behavior. We have to get it correctly because you don't fall in and out of righteousness. Let me state that again, you don't fall in and out of righteousness. Beloved, born-again believer, you can't get more righteous than you are right now.

Can you sin? Yes, absolutely! I was a teacher long ago. Do you remember what a verb is? It is an action word, right? You can do the verb, SIN: The action of sinning. Of course you can. But if you know Christ you are a saint, righteous in Christ. Sure, you can do the act of sinning, commit a sin, just don't!

"You may have a sin habit but you no longer have a sin nature." That is a great Graham Cooke quote.

Now look at the answers you wrote down. What makes a sinner a sinner? The answer is: Adam's sin. What makes a righteous man righteous? The obedience of the one man, Jesus.

The truth is when Jesus is living in you through Holy Spirit. And by the way, he is a Holy Spirit and ungodly spirits don't wanna hang around as much. So we must stay rooted in who we are. We don't come in and out, in and out, in and out of righteousness.

I like to declare: *I am the righteousness of God in Christ Jesus!* 2 Corinthians 5:21

We rely on what Christ Jesus has done for us. We put no confidence in human effort. Philippians 3:3b NLT

Your standing is righteousness, it is not based on your effort, performance or striving and it doesn't shift or change. That is your position. That may or may not be a new concept to you but many find it difficult to grasp. Some even resist it.

God made him who had no sin to be sin for us, so that in him we might become the righteousness of God. 2 Corinthians 5:21 NIV

Let me also mention what Paul wrote in Romans 10:3-10:
For they being ignorant of God's righteousness, and seeking to establish their own righteousness, have not submitted to the righteousness of God. For Christ is the end of the law for righteousness to everyone who believes.

Your sanctification is being perfected as you are becoming all of who you are. You are more and more being conformed into the image of Christ. He is the first-born among many brothers. That's you! You are a royal priesthood and holy nation, a person belonging to God.

Your righteousness and *saint thinking* is key, even central to knowing who you are in Christ. It forms your identity. Awaken to the reality of the truth, as a believer in him, your righteousness is settled. You call yourself a believer not a doubter, right? Then walk in the authority of all that has been won for you in Christ, it is an absolute game changer! I like to tell people when the church, God's called out ones, really grasps this and moves out of the pew and into the dark world as the shining ones…GAME OVER!

Chapter 22
What Stinks?

One time I came home and entered the house from our garage door. The minute I walked in, I was assaulted by a horrible odor. Even though I couldn't stand it I tried to find where the smell was coming from. No matter where I went or what room I was in I could smell the stink! I started a series of things. First, I took out the trash. I replaced the bag with a clean one. But the smell lingered. *Yuck! What in the world is that smell?* I knew I had to find the cause of the problem.

So I cleaned out the pantry, looked in every nook and cranny to see if there was a rotten potato or something that had, through neglect, turned into a science experiment. You know what I mean, right? Can you relate? Something, soft, all moldy with too many eyes. I looked in and sniffed each shelf, cleared each one and wiped them down completely, but I did not find anything. It was great to have the pantry cleaned out. I had items with expired dates for sure.

WOW! Gross! What stinks? The smell just wouldn't go away, it was so horrible, clearly a noticeable odor every time we entered our home. YUCK! It was so bad! So, I decided to go inspect the refrigerator next. I cleaned out the fridge... in a deep cleaning fashion, I took even the glass shelves out, washed them off in the sink, cleaned out the hardware metal racks of every shelf and each bin one by one. Did you know that all the shelves and glass pieces pop out? It is amazing!

I cleaned everywhere because SOMETHING was stinkin'. Next, I began to go through every item in the refrigerator. Each condiment, each bottle of dressing, and every container with leftovers. EVERYTHING to find what could be causing the problem.

Finally, I found the culprit!

Inside a blue oval, small, plastic "GLAD" container was the remainder of about half a can of black beans, which were longer black, but slimy, silvery blue and I was no longer "GLAD" I had the container. I must mention, that I have a really high gag reflex, I am extremely sensitive to smells.

My daughter Grace, when she was little would often say to me when something was malodorous "Mom, just smell your wrist; smell your perfume!" She did that because she wanted to alert me to prevent me gagging and even possibly puking in public bathrooms for example.

So the moment I even thought about opening this container's lid, I started to gag! I decided I couldn't open it even ever so slightly, with just the thought, I tossed my head back a bit as I started to gag and choke almost to the point of vomiting! So, I didn't even open the lid. I just flew hurried out of the kitchen, ran down the steps, out to the garage, where I threw the container directly into the trash the way a basketball player makes a slam dunk. All while gagging, choking, and tearing up as I tossed it. Oh, man! That little odor bomb really made a stink in the whole kitchen and even the entire house.

Later, I reflected on the impact of those slimy, rotten, black beans that had gone bad. Absolutely foul, gross! I realized that anything sinful or selfish or wrong thinking in my life or in the life of anyone, even yours, can be the source of what is really stinking up life. I was thinking about how this stinky source affects everything around it whether it be a stinky attitude or the stench of unforgiveness, complaining, unbelief, anger or rage. A little hidden source of STINKIN' THINKIN' could be as simple as wrong thoughts about ourselves, or about God or our standing with God or our identity.

Just like the small container of black beans I found on the refrigerator's top shelf began to stink up the whole house! Everything else in our life gets an awful whiff of it too. Whatever the source, it affects our entire life. And left undetected, it can really stink up our families, marriages, neighborhoods, relationships, social settings, church gatherings and our true identity. Stinkin' thinkin' may even ruin a career or our dreams and life purpose. It certainly affects our thoughts about ourselves and about Father God. Our thoughts need to be in check. We must take every thought captive.

Colossians chapter 3 tells us us how there's certain things that we need to put on and take off and other things that we just need to kill... Put to death. Anyway, I knew it took an extreme measure for me to find the stinky source. I really had to do some searching! I began to think about Psalm 139:24, 25. *Search me, O God and know my heart; Try me and know my anxious thoughts. See if there is* ***any offensive way*** *in me, and lead me in the way everlasting.* Emphasis mine.

I don't know about you, but I often need to be searched by God who is a loving Father. I know I don't necessarily detect my own short falls or sins. Think about it, the person with bad breath doesn't always know it or the one with body odor may not detect their own stench. So let me ask you... Do you need God's search? Is there an area in your life that seems to be stinky?

I don't ask out of shame or condemnation but for examination. Maybe you aren't even sure what is really bugging you or stinking things up…
Is it:
A bad attitude? A spirit of complaint? A religious spirit? A critical spirit? A loss of joy? Or perhaps you are still thinking you are a sinner, weak worms of the world when you are saved by grace. Hold on because you can't think that way when Jesus has paid for your salvation worth his blood.

He says you have been transferred from the dominion of darkness into the kingdom of light and you get to shine. So we've gotta get rid of our stinking thinking. It is a big deal to completely adopt and accept and take as your own what Jesus paid for. It's a really big deal! He called you a masterpiece. You can't keep that stinkin' thinkin'. Throw it OUT!

Let me ask you believer, do you believe? Are you still focused on being a sinner rather than a saint and a royal priest? Are you placing more emphasis on and putting more stock in the activity of Adam in your life than what the one man Christ did on your behalf?

Even is you are still not sure what the problem is, ask God to help you find the source of the stink. Stop and pray. Holy Spirit help me find the source of any STINK in my life.

Is there a situation that seems to have polluted you? Remember, that's not who you truly are. Believer, you are a blood bought saint a child of the living God. If you feel polluted or like something is made you unclean, why don't you ask the Father to search to find the rotten black beans of sin or your own stinkin' thinkin' now?

Then ask him to take it out and throw it away in the garbage. One thing I love is that God, when I've asked to be searched, has pulled out the drawers of my life, cleaned out the pantry shelves and gone straight inside the "refrigerator of my life" and when He located any stinkin' black beans, He showed them to me, all the while loving me as he does it. "Oh, baby girl this isn't you." Then he reminds me of who I am and how he sees me because of the blood of the spotless lamb, Jesus. He loves me. I am His Beloved and so are you.

This is my prayer, borrow it if you want to make it your prayer too.

Father God, thank you so much that you love me enough to tenderly search me. Thank you that as you search, you gently point out the sin or stinking thinking I've begun to believe. I repent of wrong thinking even about me that causes all kinds of problems. Thank you that you've shown me that its not my nature any longer, I am a new creation, a saint and I agree with what you say about me.

I know that if I come to you, Father, you will be so kind, thank you. Please search me to get to the problem's source and remove it from my life. Right now through confession, agreeing with you, and repentance, thinking differently on a higher level, I wait upon you Holy Spirit, in the name of Jesus I ask to be searched by you. See if there is any offensive or stinkin' way in me.

Help me to continue to walk in the way everlasting. Help me to know because of what you won for me, I am a saint and I can walk clean before you. I am one who has received the abundance of grace and the free gift of righteousness, so I can reign in life through Jesus Christ.

I receive now and believe, in full alignment with your word, that I already have and no longer need to reach or strive for the abundance of grace and the gift of righteousness. Oh, how I thank you! In the name of Jesus, Amen!

Chapter 23
When Uncertainty Creeps in - Trust!

When we can confidently arise and shine it's a sign that our identity is secure. This is occurs when we know whose we are too. When the uncertainties of life hit us, we rely on the nature and character or our loving Heavenly Father. We believe his word and we rehearse what we know of him. We have to get to know him and build history with him so we can better trust him when uncertainty creeps in!

He is always up to something good even when I can't see it.

Psalm 139:16 *Your eyes saw my unformed body;* ***all the days ordained for me were written in your book before one of them came to be.*** Emphasis mine.

Part of my day went according to plan. I left the house and had meetings with lovely people, just like I planned. CHECK! But my day unfolded in ways I never knew it would. NOT according to my plan. W*hat's going on here, God? Wanna show me what you're up to?* When this "off script" stuff happens, I have to ask, "*Whose plan did I think would be carried out anyway?*" When I don't understand what's going on or I can't see God's hand, does it mean He isn't working? No!

It makes me think of watching a play in the theater! Something about seeing a play live delights my heart. Every aspect I find exciting. I like to get dressed up, drive with my hubby to the theater, locate my seat, hold the playbill, read each actor's bio and dedication. I intently listen to the music and the way each line is delivered by the actors, all of it is great fun.

I'm amazed at the clever ways lights create mood and sets are designed. I enjoy watching the stage crew change the sets between scenes. The stage hands, dressed in black, appear as one carries out an end table, another a lamp and plant to set on the table. Then, right before my eyes, they both carefully lift and remove a small couch and turn the space into a peaceful bedroom.

Long ago, this was not the method of changing sets. Instead, at the end of the act the curtain closed which blocked the view of the stage from the audience. The orchestra played music during the set changes which made it difficult to hear any movement from behind the curtain but I sat and enjoyed the orchestral music. Once the set changed, the music faded, the curtain opened and voilà! Dramatic set changes were revealed, complete with elaborate backdrops as actors delivered their opening lines.

Which method of set transformation do I like better? Do I prefer it when I'm able to see the set change right before my eyes? Or do I like it when the theatre goes black, time lapses and finally the curtains are drawn back revealing the transformation? I'm not sure. When I think about the movement, the drama and progress of my own life's story isn't what I planned. The encounters, learnings, twist and turns, even the trials that happen make me want to peek behind the curtain to see what's going on. That's where the trust comes in.

I guess I don't like being in the dark. When I wonder what God is doing, the control freak part of me kicks in. There's this "perceived sense of comfort" which comes from knowing what is going on and what God's up to. I'd like to peek behind the curtain at what's happening during each day or season of my life. But I'm learning every day is ordained for me and what God has planned for me is good, so I'm learning to trust because he is working even when I don't see it.

It's at those times when God seems to close the curtain and it requires trust that he's always working. I was reading from the book of John with a mentee one day. She read aloud chapter 5:17 *But Jesus answered them, "My father is working until now, and I am working."* That line of scripture jumped off the page and my spirit responded. I realized a fresh God was telling me specifically, *it doesn't matter what you see or don't see Rachel, I'm always working!*

Yes, there are times when I worry, fret, get concerned or wonder about what He's up to. When I question His timing and his plans or even become frustrated in the waiting, I think about His character and the closed curtain in a theatrical production and all the movement behind before the big reveal. During a time when uncertainty creeps in, I do what King David did. He said he strengthened himself in the Lord. So, I rehearse what I know is true and I rest on his promises, I even preach to myself. Whenever I'm tempted to fret I have to think about the nature and character of God:

- He is gracious
- He is for me not against me.
- He is good.
- He loves me with an everlasting and an unending love.
- God does not change.
- He cannot lie.

These things are true for you too. *Yet the LORD longs to be gracious to you; he will rise to show you compassion. For the LORD is a God of justice. Blessed are all who wait for him!* Isaiah 30:18

Remember, He's always working. Perhaps you don't see Him at work in your current situation. I'd like to encourage you with this thought, I believe He's working both behind the curtain and right in front of you. He combats any discouragement from uncertainty, when we come to him.

His compassion and encouragement may manifest in the simplest things:

- He allows you to meet a friend
- you receive a call from your sister
- you laugh along with a cousin about a joke
- He allows you to be affected by a song lyric
- He meets you in times when you opened His word, the Bible.
- You let the rain fall on your face.
- The sound of a child's giggle

Yes, in a myriad of ways He speaks. His care and character will combat any uncertainty that creeps in, if we come to Him. So when things don't go according to plan, remember God is not shocked, scratching His head, surprised, or frustrated. No, He is working on our behalf and He rises to show us compassion.

Chapter 24
He Paid for It

When Christ completely identifies you the enemy can't any longer. GAME OVER! Like I stated earlier, it's a big deal to completely accept and claim as your own what Jesus paid for. It's a really big deal! It's a game changer. Let me illustrate.

When I am with my sisters or girlfriends we sometimes shop. I want to tell you about a time when I was *"up north"* as people in Wisconsin call it. I was up in Door County, Wisconsin with some girlfriends and just like when I'm with my sisters, we can shop till we drop! On most of my sister weekends we've made it a practice to keep a black Sharpie marker handy so we can write our names on all the bags. It is so much fun!

We mark each bag, with our name after leaving each thrift store, consignment shop, or special boutique in order to keep straight who bought what. This made for easy identification and quick retrieval later. When I went with my girlfriends *"up north"* no one had a Sharpie with them. Well, that's a major violation because one should always have a sharpie with them along with dental floss.

After our day of shopping, I opened my girlfriend's SUV back hatch, SLOWLY as contents may have shifted during travel. I looked at all the accumulated things. *Wow! This is from just one day.* We hit the candy store, favorite shops, boutiques, thrift stores and a few restaurants too. I began to open the bags to peek inside. I identified whose items were in which packages and then handed them out. "Jan you're the one that bought the soaps, so these are yours. But the towels are not." So I handed the bag containing towels to another girl friend.

Quick question. As I looked in each bag, do you think I would ever take the ones containing things my girlfriends had purchased? Would I ever take their bags home? No! I wouldn't do that! Stay and track with me here. Why wouldn't I take the bags filled with their items? Because…They paid for their stuff! Right? It belongs to them not me! I would say, "No, no, no that's yours you paid for it! You paid for it you get to have it and you own it.

Yet I've noticed, in the Christian life, many people, perhaps even you tend to carry around life's baggage, the really hard heavy stuff. All these bags are weighing us down yet it's the very thing that Jesus paid for.

We have no business carrying them around. It's not ours. It's his! He paid for it. I think He wants his stuff back and He should get the reward for everything He purchased. I think He wants the anxiety that we are carrying around. He paid for it! I think He wants the fear to go! Because Jesus hung on the cross for it and purchased the peace to replace it. He paid for our right relationship with the Father.

He wants us to never embrace stinking' thinkin' nor be okay with it. That is NOT your bag to carry. Remember your mind informs your heart, your heart informs your behavior not the opposite way around.

Sometimes we expect others to get their act together. "*Would you just get your act together! You can't seem to get it together!*" But you can't get your act together until you get your mind set right. It's all about the mind and our beliefs. That is why Scripture warns us… Do not be conformed to the patterns of this world but be transformed by the renewing of your mind.

So you've gotta know what you know in your mind. I say, mind your mind. Renewing your mind and awakening to the truth of who we really are is powerful for change. In fact, it's a game changer…Game over! That's why, in Chapter 8 I had you confess aloud the truths from the bookmark. Yes, prophesy over yourself. Declare them out loud, even loudly. Because as Graham Cooke says, "Your confession describes you, your declaration elevates you and your proclamation empowers you."

That's why we declare things, decree thinks, we agree in faith about these truths and the promises of God. That's why we say things aloud. Roman says: *Faith comes by hearing and hearing the word of God.* We increase our faith as we speak the word of God and our hearing helps us as we say it. You hear your own voice with your ears. Faith does come by hearing that Jesus died on the cross and he paid for every sin of yours. Therefore, you don't need to live in condemnation.

So you can believe in the death, burial, resurrection and ascension of Jesus Christ. Scripture says in Ephesians 2:5, 6 "…*it is by grace you have been saved. And God raised us up with Christ and seated us with him in the heavenly places in Christ Jesus,*"

Accept this and believe you are raised with him and sit with him in heavenly places! That's where you are and it's good news.

But your faith also comes by hearing you speak truth over your life, and about yourself, and about your legacy, about your children and about your future! Do you understand? It's important for us to declare things out loud because our own faith is affected by what we say.

Try these declarations... say them aloud:

- *I'm no longer called forsaken or desolate my new names are Hephzibah and Beulah he delights in me and I married him.*

- *I can do all things through Christ who strengthens me.*

- *I'm forgiven*

- *I'm lavishly loved*

- *I have a future and a hope.*

- *He's the shield around me and the lifter of my head!*

I've prayed for many people, it's such a privilege. Sometimes I've said those things, that you just said aloud, as I've prayed. Why do you think I would say those things in my prayer? Because these bedrock truths are in me, I believe them and they come bubbling up when I pray. Because faith comes from hearing, and hearing the word of God. The river is within and flows out.

So you cannot get this sense of secured identity, by just hoping for it. It comes as a by-product of being in His presence and reading the Word or sitting in the secret place with him. It is a result, it doesn't just happen.That would be like me wanting a perfect body or strong arms and pectoral muscles without ever doing a single push-up. **It all boils down to IDENTITY and with establishing yours there are no short cuts.**

Okay! You know what I' mean… It just doesn't happen. You and I have to be in the Word of God. I love the Word! It is spiritual food, it is a lamp to my feet and a light to my path.

God is speaking to us. I don't believe God only speaks to us through the Bible. Jesus is the Word. You must know that He can speak to you in so many other ways as well. I wrote about this in my book, He Speaks!

Be aware because God may speak through the watches of the night, in your dreams. He may speak to you through creation for even the stars declare the glory of God. He might even speak to you in a song's lyrics or melody; perhaps through a pastor's sermon or when you're out in nature, etc…

He can even speak when you're driving down the road, you may hear Him say, call your sister; she needs your encouragement. His voice is near. He is within you and you are hidden in him. As Graham Cooke says, "How can you get away from the one you contain?" You are God's mobile home. He speaks for sure in the secret place, it's called union.

God is still speaking! He will speak to you in the Scriptures the Word of God for sure. People say, "Well, God doesn't speak to me!" To that I would respond, "Start reading your Bible aloud, He is speaking! He's speaking to you! Remember, He's always speaking." Romans 10:17 Berean Study Bible, *Consequently, faith comes by hearing, and hearing by the word of Christ.*

So let him speak to you and speak his words back to yourself.

He speaks to you because you are his beloved and the apple of his eye.

Chapter 25
Anyone Seen My Dad? Boldly Approach

My husband worked at Sears for years. I will never forget this because Michael is a hard worker! He's an amazing and an excellent manager. While he managed a Sears store in Wisconsin, he was rarely in the office. Instead, he'd be at the auto center or maybe he'd be up and the kid's department ringing somebody up because they had a big sale or perhaps he'd be in the optical department or over in the tools department. I don't know! But when I went to visit he was rarely seated in his office. He did not sit in his office, he would go and visit all the different departments and talk to all the employees. He managed people well.

The the reason I mention this, is because our daughter, Grace loves my husband. She loves her daddy. There were days when she had him so wrapped around her little finger I'd be like "Hey, excuse me here but I'm the wife, do you know what that means? So, move over!" She and her dad are so close I'd have to wiggle my way in at times. I love their tight knit relationship.

When Grace was young, she would want to go visit her dad at the Sears store. So we'd get in the car and drive to the mall for a little shopping spree. We'd decide what we were going to do but she would want to make sure that she got to see dad at the store. It was a priority. So Grace would walk into the hub office of that SEARS store like she owned the joint.

She'd enter with such confidence, shoulders back, she'd march in and I'd be four steps behind her thinking, *Oh it's the middle of the day, we probably shouldn't bother him while he's working, he doesn't need to be interrupted by his wife and daughter.* So I cowered behind Grace who would go in so confidently. I don't know why, I was the wife!

But my daughter had zero hesitation. To this day, I still keep his Sears lanyard to remind me of the way she would approach her daddy. I kept it hanging in the closet for years, right with all of Michael's neck ties. It was a reminder of his time spent working at Sears but also for what it represented to me.

You see, the thing is, Grace would boldly walk into that hub office while I shrank back behind her a bit timid to ask for him. However, I will never forget how she'd pull open that door, only 14 or 15 years old at the time, march in, head held high, take her stance with feet planted and boldly inquire, "Anybody seen my Dad?" Heads would turn and people working would stop what they were doing and would hop to it. Because Grace had **confidence in her relationship** and carried special authority, the kind that was boldly declaring, *I'm his daughter and I'm here to see him!*

I'm not kidding or exaggerating, all of those Sears office employees would come out of their little cubicles, they'd get on their walkie-talkies, trying to locate Michael for her. They'd ask "Where is Michael?" Or I'd hear, "Hey, this is Sue, anybody know where Michael is? Is he in the auto center? Will someone please find Michael? Tell him his daughter is here to see him. Please have him to come to the hub-office, because Grace is here!"

You see, it was quite evident that she knew she had favor with her daddy. Grace was confident she'd be welcome in his office and at his place of employment and in his presence. Does that make sense? She had this confidence because he told her he loved her and they'd been on many daddy-daughter dates and fostered this sweet connection. She fully believed his love for her was genuine, complete and deep. She never doubted it. She trusted no matter what was going on in her life she'd have dad's ear. He loved his little girl so much and he still does. Do you see now, why Grace came so boldly, with confidence? Is this how you feel about Father God?

Scripture says: *Let us then approach God's throne of grace with confidence, so that we may receive mercy and find grace to help us in our time of need.* Hebrews 4:16 NIV. Yep! We can boldly approach because our righteousness and identity is found fully in Jesus.

However, some people may hesitate or won't approach because of believed lies or stinkin' thinkin', *No, no, no, you only see my sin, so I can't come very boldly into your presence.*

And God says, *"Don't you know I don't see your sin because of what Jesus did for you? It is covered by the blood. So please come, come straight to me and get the grace and the mercy that you so desperately need. I invite you to come."*

Would you agree you need some grace and mercy in your life? Yeah, I need a dump truck load of mercy and a big ole umbrella of grace over my head. I'm so grateful for it! Mercy = not treating us as our sins deserve or repaying us according to our iniquities. GLORY! I feel like shouting! God's mercy is so good!

It's vital to our identity to know and believe we may BOLDLY go to the throne! Because of the blood of the Lamb, Jesus and the finished work on the cross, we approach. It's where we get the grace and mercy we desperately need and the best news is it's already been purchased for us! And BONUS, he is inviting us to come! We get to come boldly, into his presence, to the throne. It's a really big deal! We have the privilege of knowing the King of kings and be able to approach a holy God with confidence because of what was already purchased for us. We don't have to strive or perform, we are accepted in the beloved. So, be loved.

But we will **not** go boldly to his throne if we believe that we are wretched sinners and Jesus hasn't really paid for our life or our sins. STOP THAT! That is stinkin' thinkin'! And that kind of thinking is why we hesitate or won't go to the throne in the first place. We become paralyzed by this poison and it shakes our identity and we land in unbelief. Maybe we think we'd be embarrassed if we approached, feel dirty, or unsure of how much condemnation we'd receive if we dared approached His throne. That thinking is NOT from God.

God, through Jesus, already paid for your rights, privilege, and access to the throne. It is all because of our relationship with him and new nature which is hidden in Christ, so go, boldly. *There is therefore now no condemnation for those who are in Christ Jesus.*

By the way, before the foundation of the world the blood of the lamb was spilt. Before there was a problem, God already had the solution in mind. It's vital, crucial, necessary and very important that we declare truth over our lives and believe the truth of who we are, children of the Most High God. Because that's our true identity.

We are saints, living under the blood of the spotless lamb, we are in the new covenant, the one with better promises and a better sacrifice, it tells us this in the book of Hebrews. Aren't you thankful? We are now awakening to the truth of who we really are…the BELOVED! We get to simply be loved. This is thinking clearly and it's a game-changer.

It's time! It is truly time we stop listening to the lies and get rid of any negative, performance law-based, stinkin' thinkin!' I've heard a comment about the believer's identity said this way, **when Christ completely identifies you, the enemy no longer can**. I want to have you read that again. Ready? **When Christ**

completely identifies you, the enemy no longer can. It's like... Game over!

We get to approach the throne and step up, embrace, partner and only agree with what scripture says about us. We can arise and shine! It's what Jesus purchased for us on the cross and I believe He should get his full reward, ALL that He paid for on our behalf.

Chapter 26
Righteous Standing - Blameless

Let me ask you a question, can an **unrighteous man** do a righteous act? What would your answer be? Yes/No?

Well, yes! For example, there could be a guy who, doesn't know Jesus, who has not yet been born again, whose life has not been translated from the dominion of darkness into the kingdom of light and this guy could perform a righteous act like, buying his wife flowers or something kind like that, right?

The **unrighteous man** could do a righteous act, sure! Does that act make him then, righteous? No! We understand that. We've got that part figured out. We know we stand before God blameless not by works of righteousness but because of God's mercy to us.

But, I've noticed it's the flip side where we can easily get hung up.

So, let me ask you another question. Can a **righteous man** do a sinful act? Yes/No?

Yes! But does it then make him a sinner? No! He only did the **verb** of sinning, he has not become the **noun**, sinner. Why? Because he is a righteous man we need to understand that it's because of his positional placement in Christ that he is righteous in life. I often confess aloud, "I am the righteousness of God in Christ Jesus."

Regarding our nature, we've been given a new nature. The old has gone, BEHOLD the new has come. The sanctification process is where God is making us more and more like him not us striving to please him. Let me give you a verse that sure helped me understand how much of our sanctification is God's job.

Now may the God of peace himself sanctify you completely, and may your whole spirit and soul and body ***be kept blameless*** *at the coming of our Lord Jesus Christ. He who calls you is faithful;* ***he will*** *surely do it.* 1Thessalonians 5:23, 24. NIV emphasis mine

But the righteous standing we have, our new nature, is secure and has been established by God through Jesus Christ. You've got to get this. You don't fall in and out of your righteousness. This fact really needs to be secure and settled in your thinking and beliefs because that's where your identity comes from.

As a man thinks in his heart, so is he. Proverbs 24:7 When you have that identity set you'll be able to understand yourself and even help other believers embrace that truth. So we need to know whose we are and we need to know who we are as well. And sometimes knowing who God is helps us frame that.

Regarding our righteous standing with God because of Christ, let me include a section of the devotional from Morning and Evening by Charles Spurgeon. Morning, April 4.

For our sake he made him to be sin who knew no sin, so that in him we might become the righteousness of God. **2 Corinthians 5:21.**

Mourning Christian, why are you weeping? Are you mourning over your own sins and failings? Look to your perfect Lord, and remember, you are complete in him. You are in God's sight as perfect as if you had never sinned; more than that, the Lord our Righteousness has clothed you with a royal robe of righteousness, which is wholly undeserved — you have the righteousness of God. You who are mourning by reason of inbred sin and depravity, remember, none of your sins can condemn you. You have learned to hate sin; but you have also learned how that sin is not yours — it was laid upon Christ's head. Your standing is not in yourself — it is in Christ. Your acceptance is not in yourself, but in your Lord; you are just as accepted by God today, with all your sinfulness, as you will be when you stand before His throne, free from all corruption. So I urge you, take hold of this precious thought — ***perfection in Christ!*** *For you are "complete in him." With your Savior's garment on, you are as holy as the Holy One.*

"Who is to condemn? Christ Jesus is the one who died — more than that, who was raised — who is at the right hand of God, who indeed is interceding for us."

Chapter 27
Get off the Porch - God is Not Mad at You

When I was a little girl, growing up in Iowa, we played a game outdoors, called: *Ghosts Come out at Midnight.* I was a fast little runner and I loved playing that game. It's just a simple game of tag. The rules, as I remember them: You have to go sit on the front porch if you are tagged. Our small concrete two step front stoop or the porch, is like the penalty box, that's the bad situation, you're STUCK there, trapped… *You go sit on the porch!*

In this game, whoever is "IT" runs around as fast as they can in both the front and backyards to tag as many people as possible. They win if they get everyone on the porch. When any kid is tagged they must sit on the porch. The only way those sitting on the porch could get off, is if they are "set free," touched by someone who is also free.

So anyone who is not "IT" had the ability to go to the porch, touch the shoulder(s) of whoever is stuck there. Once touched, the kids who remain on the "porch prison" are immediately FREE and they're able to join the game and run gleefully around the yard again. Does this make sense to you?

Ghosts Come out at Midnight, is what we called it. But you've probably played something similar. Here's the reason I mention this game, it relates to our identity and knowing who we are and living in the freedom of the finished work of the cross. Awakening to the truth of who we really are in Christ is crucial to being one able to assist others in freedom. I believe there are people on "the porch" of penalty or prison who are sitting there STUCK. They sit there bound by shame, condemnation under the law and many are without the hope of freedom.

I know STUCK people on the porch, so to speak, I have them in my life and I believe they're in your life too. So what do we do about this? When we awaken to who we truly are in Christ then we are the ones who get to go free them. We've got good news to share. Y*ou too can get off the porch*. You can get out of the penalty box. You can be free! If anyone sits on the porch and feels disqualified, covered in shame, condemnation, even those who are STUCK in self-righteous religion… we get to go to the porch and let them know, *no, no, no, you don't' have to stay here, you are free in the name of Jesus!* And then we get to run around the whole yard together, metaphorically speaking. We are liberated and we LIVE. We arise and we shine and we run free!

I'm sure you've heard the phrase: *hurt people, hurt people*. Or maybe, *healed people, heal people.* But I believe, *free people, free people!* We get to help people get off the porch. When our identity is secure in Christ we can help others either get to Jesus or know who they are in Christ. I think God put me on the planet hoping that I will take seriously my role to free those STUCK on the porch.

I hear him say, "Rachel, Go!"

And I get to tap people and say, "You're really, really free!" You don't think you're free, you may not feel free because of your stinkin' thinkin' or religious mindset, but I say, "Go! You are free in the kingdom!" And you're free to go around and touch other people too. That's exactly what I think my job is, to get as many people off the porch as possible! I'm hoping this book will aid in this process and my purpose.

Would you admit that sometime in your life the enemy has convinced you that even though Jesus blood was spilt for you, even though you accepted that, somehow you felt disqualified and needed to go sit on the porch. Has that happened to you, dear reader?

God is a God who is incredibly gracious. I'd like to list a couple of scriptures here that frame who God is because it's important for us to know whose we are and it helps us know who we are. It's important we know that he is keeping his promises. I love to review the promises of God. I have promises on cards on a ring and I review them all the time when I'm on my walks. Here's a promise of God that changed my life: *God is not a man, that he should lie, nor a son of man, that he should change his mind. Does he speak and not act? Does he promise and not fulfill?* Numbers 23:19. NIV

You see, God is not a man who says one thing to you one day and then can't keep his promise the next because he ran out of funds, or the ability, or he didn't know what to do because he ran out of wisdom. That's not God! Does he speak and not act? Does he promise and not fulfill?

The answer to those questions is no! **Any promise God has made to you he is able to keep.** Doesn't that make you wanna open the door, boldly with confidence and walk in and say, "Anybody seen my Dad?" just like Grace did at the Sears hub office?

You can have confidence. He said he's gonna be with me and I need him now. He said he will comfort me and I need that now. And he says that he goes before me and I need him now. Does this make sense? He speaks and he acts, he promises and he fulfills!

Here are a couple other promises for you:
But you, O Lord, are a compassionate and gracious God. Slow to anger abounding in love and faithfulness. Psalm 86:15

Maybe you think that God is mad at you. That is not so. He is slow to anger. He abounds in love.

God is not mad at you! Listen to his voice and the voice of this covenant promise, it's just like the covenant God made with Noah when he said he would no longer flood the Earth and he put a rainbow in the sky. I'm sure you're familiar with that covenant, right?

Here's what he says: *"This is like the days of Noah to me: as I swore that the waters of Noah should no more go over the earth, so I have sworn that* ***I will not be angry with you****, and I will not rebuke you."* Isaiah 54:9 ESV. emphasis mine.

Here's another one: *Your love, O Lord reaches to the heavens your faithfulness to the skies.* Psalm 36:5

He has not run out of love for you. He's not tired of you. He is not mad at you. He's not stingy and doesn't say, *you can't come to the throne of grace again, you're double dipping, you can't get another dip of grace and mercy. I'm not gonna give you any grace and mercy this time. Run along, run along,* He's not like that! Even if you had a dad who said, "No, you run a long, or get lost!" That is not our God's voice and it's not the nature of our Father God. He is slow to anger and abounding in love.

I like this quote by Graham Cook: "When God grants you a promise, he expects you to take him for granted."

Let me list another promise: God will forgive you! *If we confess our sins he is faithful and just and will forgive us our sins and cleanse us from all unrighteousness.* 1 John 1:9 It's important that we know that he's cleansing us.

Remember, God is going to complete his work in you. Here's another promise to take to the bank.

For those God foreknew he also predestined to be conformed into the likeness of his son. That is sanctification. Becoming more, and more, and more like him *that he may be the first born among many brothers* Romans 8:29.

It's important for you to know whose you are. It says in John 15:8 *This is to my father's glory that you bear much fruit showing yourselves to be my disciples.* So we don't have to shy away from getting glory because we're going to give glory. And he knows that it is his and it is from him.

Chapter 28
Hearing Voices?

My sheep hear my voice; I know them, and they follow me. John 10:27

Everyone hears voices. I wrote in another chapter about the importance of recognizing the source of the voice. Now, I'd like to share a story that helped solidify in my heart the verse from chapter 10 of the book of John. *My sheep hear my voice; I know them, and they follow me.*

I was fascinated, one time looking on Instagram, Facebook or maybe YouTube I can't even keep them all straight. Anyway, somehow I viewed a video of a huge field with sheep in a meadow, but all of these sheep were from different shepherd's flock's. Yet they all occupied the same field.

These sheep were all just hanging out, doing sheep stuff. What happened next amazed me. It was so cool! One shepherd came up and stood on a fence or rock barrier in front of all the sheep and called to his sheep.

From all the sheep, only that particular shepherd's sheep, the ones from his own flock came when he called. They followed him because they knew him and followed his voice. They're accustomed to it. They followed him because of his voice. I watched amazed, as each shepherd after shepherd called out to his sheep and only the particular sheep from his own flock followed him.

I was fascinated because I always knew sheep followed their shepherd but what I didn't know is that different herds of sheep may all lie down together in the same big field. Why am I saying this about sheep? Because you know the voice of God. He speaks! The more you read his word, the more you'll know the voice of God. And as a byproduct the more you'll talk to him and trust him.

When my mom calls me and says, "Rach, this is mom! I don't have to wonder, *who is this?* I know the minute she says "Rach," I know it's my mom's voice. Michael's mom, passed away, but she was a tiny sweet Chinese woman who was always all dressed up, sporting her bling too! She often wore a fur coat. But if she called me on the phone I didn't need to see her coat or her jewelry, it was her voice I recognized. She would say, "Hello, Rach-o" as if my name ended with an O. I knew it was Anna's voice. She'd say, "Rach-o, dis is Anna!"

Now, if I answer the phone and somebody says, "Hey babe!" It's always going to be my husband. If it isn't, then something's up and I'm in trouble! That would not be good. Right? But when he says, "Hey babe," I immediately know it's my husband, because I recognize his voice.

By the way, my sister Barb, the one whose tights got stuck on the way to the funeral, she says, "Raaaaach, it's BARB call' meeee back." Whenever she leaves a message, trust me, I know it's Barb. Why? Because I know her voice.

When my girlfriend originally from India calls, I know her voice, we have led Bible studies together for many years and we have spent a lot of time together. I love her, she's fabulous. And she's left me voicemails. But she would leave a message, "Rrrachel Shanthini haaeere!" The minute she said my name, I knew who it was without her identifying herself. Why am I saying all this?

Because when you have a voice that comes in and you hear it, **you've got to know who is speaking to you.** You have to recognize the source and ask, *Am I going to follow this voice? Should I?* The Scriptures say, *my sheep hear my voice.* Whose voice is it? If it's the voice of a stranger, I shouldn't follow it. If it's the voice of the enemy I have to **recognize, reject, repent, renounce and replace!**

It sure does matter whose voice were listening to. To better know God's voice, remain in his word and trust him to reveal to you his sound, his character, his nature and his ways.

I hope who you are is getting more solidified as you read this book. I believe one of the reasons I'm on the planet is to help people better understand their significance and the genius of God in them. (That's the tagline for my podcast "the real deal.") I'm here to help people find their Heavenly Father who cares for them deeply and desires for them to come boldly to the throne and enjoy unity with him.

If you do know who you are it's time to arise and shine. We get to lock arms with other believers in the Kingdom of God. We are the bride of Christ the ones God has chosen and equipped. The called out ones God is mobilizing and when he calls we'll hear his voice and we'll be ready!

If you'd like, turn back and declare **who you are** again from Chapter 8, page 55. Just know you are His sheep, you can hear His voice and He a good shepherd.

Chapter 29
Bug Guts

My son got married in the summertime, it was July so my sisters came to town to attend the wedding but came early. Barb, her husband, Craig and my sister Sharon traveled with them. We decided we would go to the Farmer's Market because we had an extra day together.

They arrived in the evening but traveling at night in the middle of the summer from Iowa to Wisconsin means there are plenty of open fields and swarms of bugs out after dark. There were bug guts all over Barb's car. Bugs on the front grill, bugs on the windshield, bugs on the wipers, bugs were plastered everywhere. Barb had a brand-new, white car at the time and she had these gross bugs all over her new car. We piled into the car so we could go to the farmer's market and I was seated in the driver's seat because Craig, her husband, gave me the keys to drive.

He said, "Rachel, you know where you're going, so you can drive." I was seated behind the wheel when Barb came out of my house and she gave me a look like what are you doing in my car you little upstart? She gave me a funny look and I held my hands up and said Craig told me that I should drive because I know where we're going. So she got in the backseat behind Craig who was sitting shotgun beside me.

We were all headed to the farmer's market, but there are so many bug guts splattered I could barely see. Barb began to rave. She talks so emphatically to begin with, but when she gets a little charged up or "hepped up" as she would say, she was raving and yes, she was hepped up! She asked in a long sustained tone, "Raaaach can you even see out the windshield?"

I assured, "Yes, Barb I can see! I mean it's got some bugs but I'll be okay."

"No, Raaach this is giving me a headache!"

Then she tapped on the seat in front of her, tapped her husband's shoulder, and said,"Craig we need to go to a gas station! Raaach, is there a gas station coming up soon?"

I reassured her and said, "Barb yes, there is! We will stop at the BP. It's not too far and on our way to the Farmer's Market."

"Oh, my heavens, I can't handle this! Raaach those bugs are on the windshield, they're on the wipe… CRAIG! We have grasshoppers and moths all over aaaand it's buuuugging me!"

I heard her lament but I just kept driving, I'm not kidding, I sort of felt like I had a toddler in the car. You know what I mean? Where you have to keep talking to them to calm them down.

I said, "Barb, seriously it's just down the road, don't worry you're safe, keep your seatbelt on, hands inside the vehicle, we will all be fine," joking with her.

"Raaach! Well, it's just driving me craaazy!" She bellowed, "It makes me feel like I'm runnin' down the street, like my PANTS are on FIRE!"

I just couldn't figure it out, I didn't get the correlation. Since I'm the youngest and she's the oldest, I wanted to respect and honor her so I said, "Barb I don't understand how that fits with any of this?"

And she replied, "Welllll, it makes sense in Barbara Jean world!"

In other words, the bugs were so prominent, it was driving her crazy and so she felt like she could just run down the street CRAZY like her pants were on fire!

Let me turn a corner here. What makes ME *feel like I am running down the street; like my pants are on fire!* is when people who love God and know God loves them, when those same ones who know Jesus, do NOT know who they are. Nor do they believe how special and significant they are in the kingdom. UGH! It makes me ***feel like I'm running down the street like my pants are on fire!*** It really does.

That's why I am grateful for this opportunity to write about our identity in Christ so we can celebrate together what God actually did for us. It's a big deal! I remember when these truths about identity were revealed to me through the Word and strong new-creation teaching. **It was eye-opening but more than that it was as if something I knew became something I was.** The Spirit illuminated truths into my heart. It was an awakening. That's why I keep using the word AWAKEN.

Something shifted when I realized I needed to change the way I was thinking. I was able to get rid of stinkin' thinking and I began to fully embrace the finished work of the cross and all Jesus had accomplished on my behalf. I wanted to make sure other people really knew who they are and whose they are.

Once this is settled, we can rest in our identity and celebrate each other because we are each amazing masterpieces of Almighty God. We are the priests and kings. We are the kings he is the King of kings over. We don't need to be insecure or in crisis about our identity. Remember we can have what I call, God-fidence.

It is such a game changer when we awaken to the truth of who we really are, the beloved. WE GET TO BE LOVED! It's like, GAME OVER! We get to arise and shine. But we won't arise or shine until we know and believe who we truly are. Yet when we do know, look out world!

It's also important that we link arms with each other and stop any competition or comparison. Instead, we can to celebrate and honor one another. When we celebrate who we are and who we've been created to be, then we find our purpose as representatives of Christ and we count it a privilege to step up!

Let's rejoice in who we are: righteous, accepted, approved, forgiven, chosen, favored and so much more all because of Christ Jesus' work on our behalf. We are the righteousness of God in Christ Jesus. We are sons of God! Let's step up! It is time. Beloved, let's arise and shine.

As it says in Romans 8:19 NIV, *The creation waits in eager expectation for the* ***sons of God to be revealed***. Even creation has been groaning. It is vital we know who we are and whose we are! Because we will be revealed.

The mature children of God are those who are moved by the impulses of the Holy Spirit. And you ***did not receive the "spirit of religious duty,"*** *leading you back into fear* ***of never being good enough***. *But you have received the "Spirit of* ***full acceptance,"*** *enfolding you into the family of God. And you will never feel orphaned, for as he rises up within us, our spirits join him in saying the words of tender affection, "Beloved father!" for the Holy Spirit makes God's fatherhood real to us as he whispers into our innermost being,* ***"You are God's beloved child!"***

And since we are his true children, we qualify to share all his treasures for indeed, ***we are heirs of God himself. Since we are joined to Christ, we also inherit all that he is and all that he has.***

We will experience being co-glorified with him provided that we accept his suffering as our own. Romans 8:14–17 TPT emphasis mine.

We are heirs of God; the sons of God will be revealed. Have we received our full acceptance? Are we, the church, waking up? Or are we orphaned and still asleep? Do we find ourselves lost in lies or misunderstandings, stuck in religion or a form of godliness? I ask because it is possible that any or all of these are like bug guts "splattered on our life's windshield" and they cloud our view of God, ourselves and our lives. It becomes the obstruction just like bugs on a windshield. We must awaken to who we truly are in Christ so we are no longer aimless, dimmed, confused or tempted to shrink back but instead, arise and shine.

Jesus gave gifts to men. To equip the Saints for the work of ministry, for building up the body of Christ, until we all attain the unity of the faith and of the knowledge of the son of God, to mature manhood, to the measure and stature of the fullness of Christ, so that we may no longer be children tossed to and fro by the waves and carried about by every wind of doctrine, by human cunning by craftiness in deceitful schemes. Rather speaking the truth in love, ***we are to grow up in every way into him who is the head, into Christ,*** *from whom the whole body, joined and held together by every joint with which is equipped, when each part is working properly, makes the body grow so that it builds itself up in love.* Ephesians 4:12-16.ESV

We must grow up into who we truly are then step up, be revealed to the dark, aching, groaning yet watching world. All of creation is waiting for us to arise and shine! We are the ones who contain the Spirit of the living God. We, beloved, are His mobile home! I like to say, we are the glow-in-the dark ones. *The light shines in the darkness and the darkness has NOT overcome it.* Beloved we are all part of the family of God and we are on the same team. It's vital that we don't oppose one another but remain unified. As the church, let us collectively mobilize, arise, shine and let's raise our hands high and say individually, “I am here God! I’m ready. I know who I am and I know whose I am. I am your child.”

Come on, **let’s go!**

Chapter 30
CELEBRATE Movement!

Comparison can be useful to attain a goal or uphold a standard to reach toward. This is splendid and I love it. But that's not the type of comparison I am talking about here. I've watched comparison erode people's identity. *I'm not like her, I wish I had, I'd like to be just like…* It's important that we don't compare ourselves to other people. Comparison can be a robber or joy, for sure!

I wear and sell T-shirts that say this on the front, **"Don't Compare, Don't Compete, Celebrate!"** This phrase has become one of my mantras. A girlfriend of mine said, "Rachel it's more than a T-shirt, a phrase or a topic you speak about, it's a movement!"

So I've called it, the Celebrate Movement. And I believe God called me to this message. You see, the thing is, he doesn't want us to compare ourselves to anybody else. We are each an original and he made us on purpose and for a purpose. We have a destiny and a purpose, we even have an inheritance. We are tied together in the Kingdom because we are family and we have a good Father.

God has each of us in a spot, there's a reason why you've studied certain things, why you've experienced certain things, even hard and painful things. There are reasons. We need to step up and not compare our life to anyone else's. It's important because social media offers us a window into people's curated photos of their lives along with a barrage of other things thrown at us so quickly it is easy to fall into the comparison trap. But we get to say, *I am who I am! And you get to be who you are and I celebrate you!*

God doesn't make mistakes or make junk! When He spun that double helix of your DNA to make you the way you're wired, it was no mistake. God loves you and he designed you to be you. So we can't compare and we don't need to compete. Regarding the word Compete, sometimes people say to me, "Rachel, I don't like that you say, 'Don't compete,' because competition is healthy and we always want to do our best." I agree! We should always do our best, our very best!

But the competition I'm talking about, however, is not in sports or games but in God's kingdom, His economy. Let me tell you why we needn't compete. You never need to compete for God's love, lap, listening ear or his resources. He listens to your prayers. He hears you. He hears everyone's prayers and invites us to call to him. See Jeremiah 33:3

You don't have to compete for a spot on God's lap or in the throne room. There's room for everyone! Come on in.

Competition comes from an orphan-mindset or poverty spirit. This spirit thinks when God gives something to one person, they've received your portion. Like God somehow, ran out! *Are you kidding me? Are you really going to choose to believe there's not enough to go around? What? What's with that thinking? It's stinkin' thinkin' and that's not a Kingdom mindset! That's not kingdom thinking! That's not God's ways! He doesn't lack.*

Along these lines of voices and spirits and competition, I heard Justin Allen say something that resonated with me on his Instagram reel:
"Did you know that moving in the favor of God is the fastest way to trigger demons of jealousy, envy, and the orphan spirit? Not only that but a religious spirit will often times empathize and align with the spirits in an attempt to delegitimize the grace of God on your life."

*"Here's the deal, the devil didn't give you favor and he can't take it away. While your peers may be connected to the blessings of God on your life they are not the source. Jealousy and envy say, 'why not me?' The orphan spirit says, 'that's not fair.' The religious spirit would agree with them saying, 'you don't deserve it!' But the blood of Jesus speaks a better word! Tune out the chatter. And tune in to the voice of the Father." *permission given by Justin Allen.*

Let me offer some related thoughts, from a small section, of Steve Backlund's devotional from Igniting Hope Ministries:

A critical spirit is fueled by insecurity, competition, perfectionism, and self-criticism. Insecurity causes us to dwell on the faults of others so we don't have to fully face our own issues. We tend to judge ourselves by our motives and others by their actions. Competition creates an "us against them" mentality, in which the successes of others are seen as a threat to our own future. Perfectionism makes us "not fun to be with" because we give little encouragement for improvements or positive steps made by others. The biggie, though, is self-criticism. This greatly feeds the critical spirit.

Any orphan mindset must go! Years ago our friends adopted two little boys from Uganda. When they first came to the US and joined the family's routines, my friend noticed a particular behavior occurred at meal times. As soon as the boys were seated at the table, immediately they grabbed the food that was set out. Whether it was a corn muffin, hotdogs, fruit or a piece of cheese it didn't matter, whatever it was, they just grabbed it. They thought, *if they didn't get theirs NOW they weren't gonna get any later.*

This type of scarcity or poverty-mindedness can fuel competition. It believes I'll have to take, demand or steal from you, I'm freaked out and upset and scarcity minded because I believe, *if you get your portion, then what do I have? I have nothing!*

But that's not kingdom thinking! God says he owns the cattle on 1,000 hills, right? He weighs the mountains on scales. He measures the waters of the seas in jars. Can you imagine the mason jar of God? He gathers the waters of the seas in jars! He is a big, star-breathing God! He's omnipotent, omniscient, self-sufficient and He has not run out of anything.

God can give to you even after he has given to somebody else. He has not, nor will He ever run out of your future portion. There is plenty to go around! There are glorious riches in Christ Jesus and God shall, *not might*, supply all your needs. HE IS ALMIGHTY GOD. THIS IS WHOSE YOU ARE. You are almighty God's child.

I will stress this! We mustn't compare or compete, we just need to celebrate! We celebrate who we are, whose we are and we celebrate other people as we celebrate the God who made them too. When we celebrate other people, it honors and helps them move forward in the Kingdom! It's amazing!

I am passionate about each person's significance and celebrating others. I have shared my mantra, "Don't compare, don't compete celebrate!" So I'd ask, "Are you able to celebrate yourself? Can you see your own significance?" If not, ask Holy Spirit now, how you are seen in God's eyes. Pause and listen. Remember Psalm 139. *You are fearfully and wonderfully made.* You must agree with God and get this truth settled in you mind, heart and believe it.
Write what you hear here:

1Thessalonians 5:11 NIV *Therefore encourage one another and build each other up, just as in fact you are doing.* It's like putting wind into the sails of another person. Celebration is so much fun and is contagious.

One of my favorite sayings is, "You go girl!" Try to say that aloud. One, two, three! "You go girl!" I'm telling you it is quite invigorating, liberating, even powerful to celebrate others. It takes the focus off you and introspection and places it on to another. Celebration is the only antidote to jealousy, envy and the poison of comparison.

Here's a simple example but let it serve as an illustration. One of my friends makes cookies and cupcakes that could win a Betty Crocker baking competition, I'm not exaggerating! But you should see my cupcakes. I mean, they're edible, but they're not lovely! And when I see my girlfriend's cupcakes, I could be defeated thinking, *Well! I don't make beautiful cupcakes or cookies. I don't measure up. I can't even do anything!* The truth is, I now have a perfect opportunity to say, "You go girl!" and mean it! That is how we celebrate.

Years ago, I was the keynote speaker at a retreat and I also attended the seminars that were offered by the other presenters. While I was seated at a round table in the back of a large ballroom to listen, I had a perfect view of my product table in the distance. I could see the items displayed: books, jewelry, notecards and my mantra T-shirts with the printed message, "Don't Compare, Don't Compete, Celebrate!"

Even though I designed the T-shirts, all of a sudden a new level of truth hit me. It's like a "light" had come on.

I realized I don't have to compare and I don't have to compete for God's love, his awareness, his listening ear, anointing, his favor and his resources at all! But I get to celebrate who God is, I can celebrate who I am because he fashioned me, and I can celebrate others as well.
Here's what it was, I had an epiphany the letters which read, *Don't Compare* and *Don't Compete* were written in white. I thought about the significance of the white lettering on the black T-shirt. I realized sitting there, I had designed these T-shirts and only ordered black ones with the shiny gold letters for the word celebrate!

I remembered a sermon I had heard where Bill Johnson said, **"You've got a call out the gold in people, rather than tripping over their dirt."**

BAM! As I sat there, I was overwhelmed by what I saw. It punctuated that exact point. I could see it, as plain as day. A black T-shirt like black dirt with big gold letters CELEBRATE!

Yeeeesssss! I thought, *Call out the gold, rather than tripping over the dirt! We all have the dirt! We all* ***know*** *we have dirt; I know it, you know it, your spouse knows it, your kids and your grandchildren and your friends know about their dirt too.* Dirt does not need to be pointed out. *BUT…Call out the gold without tripping over the dirt!* That's how to truly celebrate!

Celebration comes more easily, even naturally when we know who we are and whose we are. **I don't think we can really get to know who we are apart from knowing God.**

Remember dear reader, He is the one who loves you and made you. You are made on purpose for a purpose. He knows how you tick and why. The designer is the one who always knows the most about their own designs, right? You are made in His image and knowing what He is like and His character and nature will help inform you about who you are too. He already knows you intimately. When you get to know Him you'll find out about yourself.

For you formed my inward parts; you knitted me together in my mother's womb. I praise you, for I'm fearfully and wonderfully made. Wonderful are your works; my soul knows it very well. My frame was not hidden from you, when I was being made in secret, intricately woven in the depths of the earth. Your eyes saw my unformed substance; in your book were written, every one of them, the days that were formed for me, when as yet there was none of them. Psalm 139;13-16 ESV

Chapter 31
The Apple Doesn't Fall Far From the Tree!

I mentioned in previous chapters, when you get to know the Father you'll also learn about yourself because you are his child. You carry His DNA; you are made in the image and likeness of God. Jesus is the first-born among many brothers. That's you, a son of God. I'd like to share about my earthly dad, who is now with Jesus but I wrote this while he was still alive, so read on.

"I've got a story for you, Rachel listen to this one!" These are treasured words for me. You see when these words are uttered from my dad's lips, I know I'm about to hear something interesting, a quick one liner or a funny story. It also means there's a high probability that my dad will slap his leg, laugh along with me for a while and finally sigh, "Aw, that's a good one!" My father Richard has a masterful way of telling stories and jokes. It is an art form. I love stories! Telling them is a huge part of my speaking style no matter the size of the audience. I have my own method, yet I've learned from one of the best story tellers, Richard Heggen. It's sure true the apple doesn't fall far from the tree.

The other evening we were in a room filled with people. Richard told a few silly stories about his family of origin and growing up on an Iowa farm. He then said, "Okay, now someone else, tell us yours." He asked us to share about growing up, life with siblings or any childhood memories. It was delightful! No one was forced to share but I noticed people put their phones away and pulled up chairs as we shared randomly around the circle.

We chuckled and collected new information about each other from this precious time. It is the, dare I say, dying art of conversation and story telling. I believe people are hungry for it.

One friend drew me aside and said, "I haven't done what just happened in this circle in like…forever! Maybe I've never been part of something quite like this. My family never sat around and visited or told stories."

I do love my father's stories and his friendly manner. I like the way he speaks well of people and even about things. He'll say, "Oh, boy! She's the real deal or yeah, they're a dandy!" While growing up I'd hear him greet young ladies this way," Hello Freida!" He'd automatically say this to any cashier, waitress or bank teller. When I was a little girl I thought it odd… *Wow!* So *many women in this town are named Freida!*

I'd observe him closely as he walked up and asked complete strangers, "What's your middle name?" For some reason he'd gained a wealth of knowledge this way. He never started with the typical, Hello, I'm Richard what is your name? Where do you live? What do you do? Perhaps that's why the response was greater. Folks sensed his genuine interest in them.

My father meets people he's unfamiliar with and asks, "Where are you from? I mean your home, home." Often the most interesting information from total strangers spilled forth. They'd share where they grew up, about their family, things they enjoy doing or how they came to live wherever they presently do, all this from one of his casual inquiries.

He'd part as friends, hold up one hand, waving as he'd say, "Okay, well it was sure nice visiting with you!"

I do a variation of what my father does. I don't often ask middle names first, but like my father, I love to engage people in conversation. I call it a treasure hunt. I often find out something about the one in front of me in a line, or beside me in a crowd of people. I enjoy meeting new people too. I'm usually drawn by something I notice and then make a comment. "Hey, I love your hair cut, is it new for you? Wow! That coat color is beautiful on you or your nails look fabulous!" A friend told me, "I remember you coming directly over to me when you came to speak at our church and I thought, *why is this crazy woman asking me questions?* But I liked that you noticed me and I'm so glad we met that night."

Another quirky thing I love about my father, Richard is he can be found rubbing his knee in a circular motion on his jeans to the point that my nephew Beau once said, "Grandpa you're gonna wear a hole in your jeans if you keep doing that." As we were driving around town together on one of my parents' recent visits, I found myself waiting at a stoplight rubbing my right knee with my hand in the similar clockwise motion. My dad was riding shotgun. I gently hit his arm, got his attention and said, "Dad look at what I'm doing?" We shook our heads and both chuckled. I thought. *Boy, the apple doesn't fall far from the tree!* Yes, there are noticeable ways that I am like my father; you become like what you love.

What is true in the natural is true in the spiritual as well. We act and become like our heavenly Father as we spend time with Him. Because we are his children and the Spirit of God lives in the believer, we become like Him. Remember believer, you carry the DNA of God. You have an incorruptible seed within you. Jesus came to earth to put a face on God. He said when you see me you see the Father. Paul, writing to the people in Colossae says, "*The Son is the image of the invisible God, the firstborn over all creation.*" Colossians 1:15 Jesus shows us a picture of God. Jesus is God. I've heard it said, Jesus came to put a face on God; we get to be the face of Jesus to people.

These verses talk about how we are transformed into His likeness. We become sanctified and more like Father God, by God himself.

And we, who with unveiled faces reflect the Lord's glory, are being transformed into his likeness with ever-increasing glory, which comes from the Lord, who is the Spirit. 2 Corinthians 3:18

May God himself, the God of peace, sanctify you through and through. May your whole spirit, soul and body be kept blameless at the coming of our Lord Jesus Christ. The one who calls you is faithful and he will do it. 1 Thessalonians 5:23-24

Christ lives in you. This gives you assurance of sharing His glory. Colossians *1:27* NLT

I've asked myself and let me ask you too. Are we looking, acting and becoming like our heavenly Father? We become like what we behold, love and worship. Like me hanging out with my dad, we enjoy time spent with Him and we reflect Him. The apple doesn't fall far from the tree.

Chapter 32
Who Told You That?

I've felt very distracted and wasn't able to focus enough to write. After posting on Instagram, I was waylaid by social media and was glued, mindlessly, to my phone. *Oh, it's getting late and I'm still in my robe!* So I decided to go outside, get some fresh air and take my daily walk to clear my head. It helped awhile.

Then I made myself a delicious lunch and cleaned up the kitchen. Both making lunch and doing the dishes were a bit of a stalling tactic because I still wasn't FEELING it yet, writing I mean. But I climbed the stairs and chose to start. *It's a matter of the will Rachel.* I sat down beside my Christmas tree to gather my thoughts and began to write. I love sitting there.

I've enjoyed sitting in my upper loft with my Christmas tree lit, for weeks now. It is peaceful and tranquil and once I sit down, I never want to get up. I put the tree up early in November because I knew my December was filled with the normal activities and additional speaking engagements. I'll admit I had a little *battle in my mind* over whether or not I should put up the tree so early. The mental wrestle went something like this.

Rachel, you usually wait until after Thanksgiving to put up the tree. You should get the most out of the season of thankfulness without moving on to the Christmas season. But I am thankful no matter what month it is. I told myself. Don't rush into it. It's too early, you can't have people over in November, before Thanksgiving, with a tree up! You really can't put the tree up it's too early.

Then I heard myself ask this aloud, **"Who told you that?"** What? *Who told you that?* YEAH! *I'm free to do it if I want. NOW is when I have time. Besides, it isn't a God commandment, Rachel it is only* *your own thoughts and the influence of others around who may wonder about it…* so I decided…*I'm going to put up the Christmas tree.*

Even though it took me two or three days to put up the tree, I had a wonderful time. The outcome was splendid. A few years ago the "pre-lit" tree was no longer "lit," so I had to put all new lights on this year, 2,300 of them! But I'm glad I did it in November because I had many free days and I had a few gatherings in my home. I knew it would be good to have the warmth and the festive atmosphere for these things:

- My parents visit and "Sisters Weekend"
- Life Group
- "Salad supper and share your testimony" with ladies from Bible Study
- Prayer times with friends
- House guests for four nights
- Family Christmas
- Morning coffee with my husband before work

Let me turn a corner and have you read these words from Genesis 3:8-11a

*They heard the sound of the Lord God walking in the garden in the cool of the day, the man and his wife hid themselves from the presence of the LORD God among the trees of the garden. But the Lord God called the man and said to him, "Where are you?" And he said, "I heard the sound of you in the garden, and I was afraid, because I was naked, and I hid myself." He said, "**Who told you that** you were naked?"* Emphasis mine.

Who told you that:

- You can't put up your Christmas tree yet!
- You won't be able to concentrate long enough to get it done.

- You're not smart!
- You're too short!
- Your situation will never change!
- You're unworthy.
- You don't have a bright future.
- You're too young, or too old.
- You aren't able to do/become/have_____________(fill in the blank)

Word for the wise. It might be good for your overall identity to ask yourself, **Who told you that?**

Yeah, Rachel ***who told you that*** *you were too distracted and wouldn't finish writing this chapter?* BOOM! CHAPTER FINISHED.

Chapter 33
Nothing is Wasted

I listened to the swish, swish, swish of my slippers shuffling on the kitchen floor as I opened the microwave to warm up a cup of coffee. I drank a few sips and headed to make the bed. Later, I searched for my coffee mug and spun around a few times looking for it. *Oh, found it!* By then it was cold again. *Yikes! I should just get started.* I appeared busy, but I was simply stalling. I didn't want to face what I had on the docket for the day.

I then received a text from my cousin. I had asked her to hold me accountable to organize items so I could start the potentially painful and much-needed process of writing He Speaks.

She's excellent at reminders, better than any phone app could ever be. My cousin regularly notifies me about each resolve I have declared. Today was no exception. *Good morning Sunshine! It's your blogging day! And start making a pile of all the things you'll need to dig into in a few weeks.*

I delayed the inevitable task long enough. *Just get moving!* I rummaged through a few baskets and boxes looking for past calendars, my journals and the cards I'd received. I climbed up and down steps repeatedly during my search. I looked in coffee table drawers and on bookshelves as I gathered my journals from the last 4-5 years.

I opened each one, looked at the handwriting and began to read a few of the sections. Some sentences instantly brought me back to the preserved moment. I noticed the writing was indicative of the condition of my heart. Sometimes I wrote over the pages in all different random directions. It was as if my thoughts couldn't land in any order on the page. It was chaotic writing, but it was a chaotic time.

It was a difficult time for me and my family. This trial felt like it came out of nowhere and hit me like a Mack truck. Grief related to loss had thrown me off. These points of confusion were now preserved on paper and demonstrated through my own troubled handwriting. Sometimes large scribblings filled the pages. Each notebook contained a mixture of the following:

- personal journal
- sermon notes
- song lyrics
- my response to Bible passages
- prayers to God
- personal reflections
- questions and confessions.

No, stop reading, Rachel! Just look for the start and end dates! Then collect them and put them in chronological order. I reached in the kitchen drawer and drew out a black Sharpie marker and began to label each journal with a sticky note near the top.

I marked them all. *Phew! Progress.* I read a few of the cards I'd received. Next, I glanced at the calendars where I had recorded something I'd prayed about each day. I came to a circled date in mid September 2014. This calendar entry noted a phone conversation I had with my daughter Grace.

The conversation occurred while I was speaking at a retreat in northern Michigan. I immediately envisioned the step on which I sat in the sun. I could feel the breeze on my face. I remember I was outside my cabin when this call came in. This memory was both precious and painful to recollect. I stopped.

I had to stop and cry out to God. The memory was so vivid. It was beautiful and absolutely precious. In the "time warp thing" it felt as if it had just happened yet it seemed extremely distant like it were decades ago.

The pleasure and pain I experienced caused fresh tears to flow. *I miss her! I just miss my daughter Grace! God, I know you are good and you are in charge but it still hurts and I don't know if I can write about it today or anytime soon.*

I'm not certain how long I sat there crying but eventually I did get up. I was hungry and needed to eat lunch and possibly exercise too. I descended the stairs still in my pajamas and slippers. The familiar sound of my slippers shuffling rang in my ears. *Okay, it's no longer breakfast and coffee time. You, my dear, had better make yourself somethin' to eat.*

As I assembled a salad of fresh greens, beets, olives and chopped celery, I reached for the few remaining salt and pepper cashews I had in a cabinet. *Only a handful… Well, that'll do. Perfect! I wouldn't want to let these babies go to waste!*

I tugged on the refrigerator door and opened it with a grin. *Yay! That yummy zesty dressing I made yesterday is in here.* I had a jar of horseradish pickles, which no longer had any pickles in it, just juices, so I spooned out some stone ground mustard and added it, whisked both together and poured the mixture through a funnel into a glass dressing bottle.

Fabulous! I chuckled as I exclaimed, "I've used whatever is available today to make my lunch and along with yesterday's concoction, **I haven't wasted anything!"**

What's true in the natural is true in the spiritual! I heard my spirit agree with the Spirit of God which said, *You know Rachel, God doesn't waste anything either.* I mused. Yeah, yesterday I thought, *I can't throw away this pickle juice…it could be used for something!*

I believe God doesn't waste one day of my life, one hard thing, or one tear shed. He uses it all and nothing is wasted.

Those who sow in tears will reap with songs of joy. He who goes out weeping, carrying seed to sow, will return with songs of joy, carrying sheaves with him. Psalm 126:5, 6

You keep track of all my sorrows. You have collected all my tears in your bottle. You have recorded each one in your book. Psalm 56:8 NLT

As I finished eating my delicious salad, these thoughts came to me. *I'm glad I started organizing my journals and looking through things. You know Rachel you aren't the same person you were when you wrote on the pages of those journals all those years ago. You know more fully who you are and whose you are and you have gone through an upgrade. You have been beautifully changed and shaped by God through the hardest of times. THIS IS NOT WASTED IN YOUR LIFE.*

As I rose, so did my hope. You see, I know God:

- Is for me not against me
- Causes all things to work together for my good
- Is with me in hard times
- Is close to the broken-hearted
- Saves those who a crushed in spirit
- Is near
- Is good
- Loves me
- Is a restorer and reconciler

- Keeps my tears in a bottle
- Is a way maker
- Is a rock on which I can stand
- Has already won the battle

I fight from victory not for victory but from victory. I had to remind myself and now I'll remind you. No matter what you're facing today, no matter how long your trial or season of difficultly may be, no matter what wilderness you are walking through, remember He uses it all and nothing is wasted! Not even your tears.

Chapter 34
Doing a New Thing

Early in the global pandemic, a season of forced sabbath rest, I was seated on the couch participating in my second EVER "Zoom call" with some girlfriends. The Coronavirus (Covid-19) and the "Stay Home - Stay Safe" movement was sweeping the nation and globe. One friend posed a simple question, "How can we pray for you in this season?"

I will never forget it, because within seconds, out of my mouth tumbled, "Pray that I would use this season well and I'd get whatever God wants me to have and leave behind anything He doesn't need me to carry into the future." I've been thinking a lot about my request, it's still my prayer today.

I hear people use phrases like: *new normal, back to normal, when this is over, as soon as we can begin to live our normal lives.* I have this ache in my heart and stirring in my spirit. It's a longing of sorts because I don't want to go totally back to *"normal."* I want change to occur, by the work of Holy Spirit, in my life and be transformed by the renewing of my mind.

I want to live differently because I think differently. I desire an upgrade in my vision for my life, my future and those who live around me and are close to me. I don't want *NORMAL*. I have this sigh in my heart, *"Oh, God don't let me miss it. I want to squeeze out everything from this time you want me to receive and then give it out."* I don't want to live in fear that I'll "miss it" because perfect love casts out fear.

I feel a bit like a caterpillar that goes along eating up everything in sight as it's about to enter into the confines of the tightly bound up chrysalis stage. Even before the pandemic, I had been so HUNGRY for more of God and intimacy and fellowship with the Holy Spirit. I don't want the hunger for Him to die out like a glowing ember. Rather, I'd like it to be fanned into flame, burning ever brighter during this rest period.

As far as the caterpillar goes, I really have no idea how one feels, but I do think there are similarities here: it's dark, closed in, lonely, without contact with the outer world for a season, ten to fifteen days, then it emerges and BUSTS out to FLY!

So here are the things I pray will not effect my identity or follow me into the future as I break out of the cocoon or box:

- self-limiting thoughts
- confusion
- double mindedness
- distractions
- slothfulness
- unbelief
- fear
- dread
- pride
- judgment
- fear of man
- praise of man
- pettiness
- unkindness
- bitterness
- joylessness

Maybe you are like me. Are you amazed at how completely different a caterpillar is from the butterfly? Think about it, one is worm-like, so slow and lowly and confined while the other is beautifully ornate, whimsical and glorious not bound to land but flutters and flies and purposefully alights.

A few years back this verse became an inheritance verse for me, like God gave it to me not for a season but for an outlook on life, a perspective shift. It has helped me navigate changes that happened in my home, my church, my friendships and my family. It was a welcomed metaphor for my life's journey and it still gives me a sense of hope and excitement about the future..*do you not perceive it?* It's like I hear Holy Spirit gleefully rubbing his hands together as he bounces on his toes with joy about what's to come. *"Do you not perceive it?"* God alone is the ONLY one who can make a way in the desert and give us streams in the wasteland.

May I suggest you join me? Let's not dwell on the past or wish it would all go back to normal, rather let's welcome the "New Normal" and break out of the box and receive the **new thing** He is doing **in** us, **through** us and **around** us. Let's FLY!

Forget the former things; do not dwell on the past. See, I am doing a new thing! Now it springs up; ***do you not perceive it?*** *I am making a way in the wilderness and streams in the wasteland.* Isaiah 43:18,19 Emphasis mine.

So let's all live NOW and as we move forward here is a phrase I use in life, it's also the title of one of a talks I give. I hope this will help you too.

"Look back with gratitude and forward with faith."

As I have observed, however, my experience has been, instead of gratitude and faith, many people look back with regret and forward with fear. This pattern of thinking keeps us stuck. But God is doing a new thing and we can look back with gratitude, see what he has done in the past, which will help ground us and encourage us so we are able to look forward with faith. My hope is that God is doing a new thing even in your life as you read this book…*do you not perceive it?* A new thing with your identity as you awaken to the truth of who you are in Christ.

Chapter 35
What God is NOT Doing

Encountering the nature, character and promises of God helps shape our identity and solidify our belief in his goodness and our safety as His children. During the start of the pandemic I wrote this for my blog, "Fresh Perspectives for Everyday Life." Let me share it here.

Fear runs rampant and anxiety levels rise and many people are hooked up to news feeds like it's an IV, so I want to share a few thoughts about "What God is NOT doing!"

She was dressed for summer in an icy blue, vertically striped shirt and a pair of white pants. Her familiar smile lit up her face and mine. She greeted me with a sweet hug that enveloped me, "Hi friend!" she blurted. Then, "Oh, I have to run to the bathroom. I'll be right back!"

When she returned, we ordered our drinks, grabbed a seat and caught up. "It's been months since we last met. When was that?" we wondered. Many work transitions and family health trials have entered her life since we'd last met. I sat. I listened. She mentioned she is reading the book of Daniel now and we thought through each situation from Daniel's lens and his prayer of praise in Scripture.*

She asked, "So, what's going on with you?" I reported about some of the fun and beautiful things going on in my life and what God's been teaching me about me. I also shared a few updates related to my husband, ministry, plus a quick update on my empty nest and my grown children.

We marveled at all that had taken place in our lives while, it seemed, other things hadn't changed or shifted at all. We both have difficult situations where, since we last spoke, it seems there had been no change. **You know what I mean where it appears God is not doing anything related to an issue.** I got to thinking about that wacky perspective of concentrating on what God's not doing and how "off" and faithless and Biblically impossible that is.

So, I told her. "You know, the other day, I thought of it this way: I can only imagine what my response would be, if I had throughly cleaned my house;-vacuumed all the carpeted rooms, dusted the entire place, scrubbed every toilet, mopped all the floors, washed every dish and put them all away, only to hear my husband complain when he returned home, "You left the mail on the counter!" I'd be so disheartened thinking, *WHAT? Don't you see all the things I've done?*

"It's kind of like that." I said. "God is doing SO many wonderful things all around me and I resolve not to be the bratty kid who stomps her foot at the Father and accuses Him of inactivity. *But, but, but you haven't done…this yet, God!"*

She said, "Wow! I've never thought of it like that. Good point."

Okay, yeah, it may be tempting to think He is not at work. I've been there. So whenever I'm tempted to focus on what God is seemingly *NOT doing*, I say, *yeah, sure, God is **not** doing some things.* Here are a few of the things God is **NOT** DOING:

- He's **not** scratching his head wondering, *Oh, boy what do I do now?"* or *"How will I help?*
- He's **not** out of the office, off His throne or unaware.
- He's **not** working against me.

- He's **not** surprised or shocked.
- He's **not** wringing his hands.
- He's **not** biting his nails, bewildered, wondering, "*How do I respond in this difficult situation?*"
- He's **not** calling in a committee to help with decisions.

HE'S GOD! And He is good! I truly believe God is doing so much, in and around me, all the time! Jesus is quoted in the book of John saying, *"My father is always working."* So, yes, for now, I will live in the mystery of all He is doing. I am thankful and I praise Him and I'm thankful for the things he is NOT doing as well.

*This is the passage my friend had alluded to when we started our conversation.

During the night the mystery was revealed to Daniel in a vision. Then Daniel praised the God of heaven and said: "Praise be to the name of God for ever and ever; wisdom and power are his. He changes times and seasons; he deposes kings and raises up others. He gives wisdom to the wise and knowledge to the discerning. ***He reveals deep and hidden things;*** *he knows what lies in darkness and light dwells with him. I thank and praise you, God of my ancestors: You have given me wisdom and power, you have made known to me what we asked of you, you have made known to us the dream of the king." Daniel 2:19-23* Emphasis mine.

Beloved, during times of uncertainly, in the wondering or waiting, remember who you are and whose you are and that you are hidden in Him. He is God Almighty.

"You can go to God Most High to hide. You can go to God All-Powerful for protection. I say to the Lord, "You are my place of safety, my fortress. My God, I trust in you." God will save you from hidden dangers and from deadly diseases. You can go to him for protection. He will cover you like a bird

spreading its wings over its babies. You can trust him to surround and protect you like a shield. You will have nothing to fear at night and no need to be afraid of enemy arrows during the day. You will have no fear of diseases that come in the dark or terrible suffering that comes at noon. A thousand people may fall dead at your side or ten thousand right beside you, but nothing bad will happen to you! All you will have to do is watch, and you will see that the wicked are punished. You trust in the Lord for protection. You have made God Most High your place of safety. So nothing bad will happen to you. No diseases will come near your home. He will command his angels to protect you wherever you go. Their hands will catch you so that you will not hit your foot on a rock. You will have power to trample on lions and poisonous snakes. The Lord says, "If someone trusts me, I will save them. I will protect my followers who call to me for help. When my followers call to me, I will answer them. I will be with them when they are in trouble. I will rescue them and honor them. I will give my followers a long life and show them my power to save.""" Psalms 91:1-16 ERV

Chapter 36
Identity Self Examination

Check Yourself. I don't present these to arouse shame or heap on condemnation but the help you identify places where alignment to your true self and secured Christ-centered identity made need some additional work or Holy Spirit's tweaking.

Your identity might be in crisis:

If you live in fear of the world's influence infecting or hurting or steering you. This is a sign that you don't know who you are. In the Old Testament times, the lepers had to cry out, "Unclean, unclean!" People fled from lepers in fear. Because exposure would mean they may contract leprosy also. However, in the New Testament we see how Jesus went toward, touched and healed the lepers. The power of who He is was more powerful than what was "on them." Yes, the world maybe dark but that's when the light shines even brighter. So beloved, don't run away, arise and shine.

Be warned, your identity may remain in crisis or at least it's, as my Dad used to say, "A little shaky" if you don't want others to soar, be recognized or shine. Think about it. Do you celebrate the success and advancement of others? Can you truly say, "You go girl!" and mean it? If not, there's still more work to be done in your beliefs about yourself, your identity isn't in line with who you really are and who God says you are in the Word. But be encouraged and remember your spiritual DNA is already set and informs who you are, not your past or your performance or position amongst others in some sort of pecking order.
The validation you need is from the Lord. The joy of the Lord is your strength. Only when you believe this and receive it will you

truly walk in ***God-fidence.*** You cannot be unraveled or shaken! You stand in the One who knit you together and isn't about to let you unravel. He is the One who is the unshakable rock beneath your feet and He is for you never against you.

So, I say, "You go girl." I pray you are awakening to the truth of who you really are in Christ. Walking in a secure identity is a game changer and you become a world changer because you change the world around YOU!

Even Jesus had to answer the Devil's attacks, aimed at His identity…"*IF* you are the son of God" is how he questioned Jesus in the wilderness of temptation. The enemy wants us to doubt our identity and he wanted it to be in question for Jesus too. I love how Jesus answered Satan. He answered these attacks with the word of God which showed his true identity and God's authority. God had already told him and those around at his baptism who Jesus was. *And a voice from heaven said, "This is my Son, whom I love; with him I am well pleased."* Matthew 3:17 NIV

Your identity may be in crisis: If you feed on the praise of men and seek for their approval and crave their recognition. That is a sign your identity isn't fully awakened and secure in Christ. The insecurity points to the fact that you may still be believing lies about yourself or about God. The antidote to the crisis is to rest in His presence and be filled with the Holy Spirit. Draw near and allow Him to tell you who you truly are. Alignment will come when your thoughts and perspectives line up with the Word and His voice.

What does the Word say? I'd like to include a few key verses here to help you. You may want to declare these statements or look up these Scriptures.

- I never need to doubt my significance: Psalm 139.
- I am very loved: John 15:9; Romans 8:38-39; Psalm 103:8-14.
- I am adequate in Christ Jesus: 2 Corinthians 3:5-6
- I have the Spirit's power: Acts1:8; Ephesians 1:19
- God rejoices over me: Zephaniah 3:17; Isaiah 62:5b
- I can boldly approach my Father: Hebrews 4:16

Remember the importance of the voices in your head? The negative voices will always be tied to **your** performance, behavior, bring condemnation and ties you to the past. While the positive voice of God relates to your position in **Christ**, your identity is based on his perfect performance and His spotless behavior which makes your identity in Him secure. The positive voice talks to you about your future and your destiny which is set by God and He speaks confirmation, never condemnation. *There is therefore now no condemnation for those who are in Christ Jesus.* Romans 8:1 ESV.

Your identity may still be in crisis if your circumstance defines you and your future more than what God says. During an extremely difficult season in my life, I wasn't sure if a trial I was in would ever end. But then I heard in a message Graham Cooke gave, something that literally shifted my perspective about my own circumstance. Graham said, "If you are in Christ, so are all your circumstances!" Boom! A truth bomb went off.

Immediately, I felt God's presence in the trail with me rather than me trying to ask him to come shift/change my situation. I am in

Him and so are all my circumstances, thoughts, questions, curiosities and trials. I knew God had me. I knew and could confidently say, "He's got this." I had a shifted perspective because I didn't need to ask the Prince of Peace to come enter my circumstance, I felt him already there in it.

Examine yourself, let me ask you:

- Do you know who you are?
- Do you know whose you are?
- Do you know where you are?
- Do you still have stinking thinking?
- Whose view do you have of yourself?
- Whose voice are you listening to?
- Do you know you are a masterpiece?
- Will you cease striving to please God and rest in Him?
- Do you know what's already been purchased for you?

If you know, will you stop with the sin of unbelief? Will you agree with God on who he says you are? God has the final word, will you agree with him? Are you a child of the Most High God? If you are, thank him! Praise his name for all that he has won for you. If you've only heard about him, will you surrender your life to Him now?

We all have to answer these questions, *Who am I? Who is God?* We are incredibly powerful when we know who we are and whose we are. When we believe and can say, "I am who God says I am! Nothing more, nothing less." I will agree with what He said in His Word about me. His Word has the final word!
BOOM!

This is a game changer! Let me encourage you with this prayer from Colossians; a passage packed with truth about our identity in Christ.

COLOSSIANS 1:9-20 *For this reason, since the day we heard about you, we have not stopped praying for you. We continually ask God to fill you with the knowledge of his will through all the wisdom and understanding that the Spirit gives, so that you may live a life worthy of the Lord and please him in every way: bearing fruit in every good work, growing in the knowledge of God, being strengthened with all power according to his glorious might so that you may have great endurance and patience, and giving joyful thanks to the Father, who has qualified you to share in the inheritance of his holy people in the kingdom of light. For he has rescued us from the dominion of darkness and brought us into the kingdom of the Son he loves, in whom we have redemption, the forgiveness of sins.*

The Supremacy of the Son of God

The Son is the image of the invisible God, the firstborn over all creation. For in him all things were created: things in heaven and on earth, visible and invisible, whether thrones or powers or rulers or authorities; all things have been created through him and for him. He is before all things, and in him all things hold together. And he is the head of the body, the church; he is the beginning and the firstborn from among the dead, so that in everything he might have the supremacy. For God was pleased to have all his fullness dwell in him, and through him to reconcile to himself all things, whether things on earth or things in heaven, by making peace through his blood, shed on the cross.

I'm recapping here, but it is so important to review so that our identity is secured in truth.

These truths from Igniting Hope Ministries, I'd like to declare over you, beloved:

- You are a saint.

- You are prone to doing things right.
- You cannot help but be blessed.
- You increase in joy the more you rest in His presence.
- The Lord works powerfully through you.
- He is mighty to meet you in your time of need. He is mighty to uphold you.
- You are pure in his eyes, because of the sacrifice of his son, Jesus.

Use the mirror of the word rather than the mirror on the wall. We must distinguish the voices we hear in our heads but continue to celebrate and tune into the voice of God who actually still speaks and is always speaking. You have a good Father, God. He loves you.

We have to get rid of our stinkin' thinkin'! I've seen so many people stuck in law-based religious thinking, bound in performance mode, running around trying to please the Father, when He's already pleased! It's time to get our tights unstuck and **get off the porch! Beloved, arise shine!**

We've got to know that we can boldly approach the throne of grace. We need to know what is actually in the shopping bag that Jesus paid for. The finished work of Jesus was on the cross, he cried out, *"It is finished."*

We've got to know who we are and whose we are! Because when we know, it shows an identity rooted in Christ rather than in crisis. You've got to know who you are, whose you are and what's been won for you. When you know who you are, it makes others secure or curious. And when they see it and recognize it's real, they may ask about it. You'll become somewhat of a mooring in someone's life because of your secure and solid identity.

Remember, you are God's mobile home…Christ **in you** is the hope of glory.

When we think correctly, we will believe correctly, when we believe correctly we will behave the way God intends. You never behave your way into belief. It starts with renewing the mind. The time has come for us to know who we are and step up and be the purified bride for whom Jesus is returning.

Chapter 37
Here Comes the Bride

It all ends in a wedding! We are the bride. You've probably seen "First Look" videos from weddings. The bride is all prepared and ready, dressed with every detail and finery in place and she approaches the groom whose back is to her. She taps his shoulder to signal she is ready for his viewing. He then turns around for the "first look!" Oh, man! It gets me EVERY time.
My son and daughter-in-law have one of the most beautiful wedding videos! I've watched it over and over.

My daughter-in-law was such a beautiful, creamy-skinned, pure and lovely bride! The look of delight on my son's face when he turned around is imprinted on me. He was overjoyed. I love the part of the video where my son motioned with his raised, index finger in a twirling motion, for her to spin around. She smiled and did as he requested so he could take in all her beauty.

As he took both of her hands and drew her to himself for an embrace, she was equally joyful. We need to see ourselves in the kingdom as the pure and spotless bride that we are because of what Jesus Christ has done. We need to present ourselves to our groom in this delighted unashamed joyful way.

When I view my son's wedding video, it's the look on his face and the joy on hers, it gets me every time. The reception party is the wedding feast. Think of it in the kingdom! The wedding feast of the Lamb is ready, the banquet table is set and the banner over us is love! We can rejoice and celebrate who we are and whose we are, the beloved! So just Be Loved!

"Jesus will not carry out his purposes of grace without the bride. You are his partner and his helper, his hand and his voice upon the earth. You are called to labor in love with Jesus you are filled with the grace, anointing, and power to set the captives free." - Encounter God's Heart...Walls of Protection by Brian Simmons.

The bride, Scripture tells us, will be without spot or wrinkle and she will be without an identity crisis too. She will be the beloved one secure in her identity, her purpose, her position and authority in Christ.

I believe Jesus will come back for his bride when we're prepared. We can't be in our metaphorical bathrobes, hair in rollers, no make up on and unaware he's coming. He will return! We must know who we are and arise. We must own our authority and royalty, he is our King! Do you recall Matthew 4:17 Jesus began to preach, saying, *"Repent, for the kingdom of heaven is at hand."* Let's be ready as sons of God and the spotless bride of Christ because even creation is waiting for the revealing of the sons!

I believe Jesus will come to claim his purified bride. One of the best ways to be purified is to stay in the Word, remain connected to other believers, reject lies and believe the truth of who God says we are. We must awaken to our true identity in Christ.

Jesus will return; he's coming back for a purified bride. What an invitation! Let's be the bride that knows how lovely she is, how much she is loved and the price that was paid for her life. When we walk in the assurance of knowing who we are our identity is never in crisis it will be established firmly in Christ.

The Lord is still waiting for you to come home to him, so he can show you his amazing love, and like he promised he will conquer you to bless you. For the Lord is always faithful to his promises. Those who intertwined their hearts with him waiting for him to help them will be overwhelmed with bliss. Isaiah 30:18 TPT

Say aloud, *I am about to be overwhelmed with bliss!*

If your identity is set and you know who you are in Christ I celebrate with you. This is a big deal and a game changer in your life's identity. Praise God.

Still have questions? That's okay! Continue in the Word. I'd encourage you to ask Holy Spirit, "Show me who I am and reveal to me my true identity." No matter your stage or where you are in the process of awakening to your true identity in Christ, know it's a journey. Let me leave you with this prayer.

Father, I thank you for being our bride-groom. I thank you for this reader, you've paid a high price for each one. Thank you God for the blood that was shed so we could be called chosen, beloved children of the King of kings and the Lord of lords. I pray a blessing on this reader. I pray that when this book is closed and we go from here, we would know that we are yours and that you love us lavishly. So may we be loved in the name of Jesus, amen!

Chapter 38
Signing Off

Once we know who we are and whose we are, our identity becomes galvanized, firm and immovable. When our identity is set and we fully awaken to who we truly are, it's a game changer. GAME OVER! When this happens we can get off the porch, break out of the box, leave the pew. When we know who we are there's nothing to do but **shine**. The light of Jesus is inside the believer. *You are the light of the world.*

In the power of the Holy Spirit we are able to do whatever he sets before us to do. The joy of the Lord is our strength and he is always working for us. Years ago there was a song by The Newsboys, I think it was titled "Shine" it was loosely taken from the scripture, *Let your light so shine before men that they may see your good works and glorify your father in heaven,* from the book of Matthew chapter 5.

I'll share some of the lyrics from the chorus:

Shine, make them wonder what you've got, make them wish that they were not on the outside looking board. Shine, let it shine before men, let 'em see good works and then let 'em glorify the Lord.

You are a glow in the dark person a new creation created in Christ Jesus to do good works that he prepared in advanced for you to do. There's no need to stay inside the church shining with the church. The church gathers so that we can scatter. The church sits in the pews so it can leave them. Once you know who you are and whose you are, you are then able to celebrate God, yourself, and others. I hope you realize you are incredibly gifted and a masterpiece of God. He makes no mistakes and He doesn't make junk. He has created you on purpose, for a purpose and he wants you to shine His light that is within you, everywhere.

You are the righteousness of God in Christ Jesus. Your old nature is gone; behold the new has come. You have been moved from the dominion of darkness and transferred into the kingdom of light. You are a shining one! **When you awaken to who you really are there is no going back.** It is just like the caterpillar that has busted out of the chrysalis stage and flown away in its butterfly state, gloriously transformed, completely different.

Believing God is for you and never against you is a mindset and a lens through which you can view your entire life. God is not angry or mad at you and he doesn't rebuke or punish you. See Isaiah 54:9,10. *He has sworn to never rebuke you or be angry with you.* It says His steadfast, faithful love for you is constant and will remain. Knowing this is not as key as believing this!

My prayer is that you would realize there are so many voices in your head but when the lies come in you will recognize, reject, repent, renounce, and replace them with the truth. The truth of who you are in Christ a new-creation being. Beloved, you are a saint not a sinner. The truth is while you were a sinner Christ died for you. *For the joy set before him he endured the cross.* He saw your value, something in you that was worth dying for. Yes, you are to die for! God put you in Jesus and put Jesus in you. What an amazing double hold.

I have only wanted to share my heart, real stories and moments from my life. Family is key! That's why I write about my kids, my sisters, and why I bring my husband along with me when I speak and why he's so involved in the process of my writing too. I desire to be the real deal and because we are family, we have the same good Father. Know that I love you and God loves you. I've told stories and shared scriptures and even quoted a few songs, that's the way I roll! My prayer is you would be unleashed, in the name of Jesus, to fully be who God made you be. You are made on purpose for a purpose. You are part of the body: a hand, an eye, an ear and no one else is like you! There never has been nor will there ever be another you. You are completely unique, an original masterpiece, you are made and designed by a wonderful creator. You are God's grand TA DA!

There is no reason for you to think you're not significant because the God of the universe made you, loves you and died to allow you to experience new creation life that is abundant and full. You are crucified with Christ, buried with him, co-raised with Jesus and God has also seated you with Jesus in the heavens. That's where you are, a bi-locational being. You shine His light here on the earth and you carry His presence and fragrance, the aroma of Christ, wherever you go. You smell lovely! Wow! Christ in you is the hope of glory!

It's a game changer when you fully awaken to the truth of who you are a new creation being, set apart and dearly, lavishly loved by a good Father. I'm thrilled you have hung with me this long and have read this book to this point. I realize I have been repetitive, but it is purposeful for the truth to be emphasized and embraced and I certainly hope it has encouraged you.

I'm signing off now, as I go know this: I celebrate your significance and the genius of God in you. So go be "the real deal!" You've got this and God's got you!

Be loved! Beloved, arise shine!

Appendix

When I was at Global Awakening for GSI, Global Summer Intensive, in 2019, Mike Hutchings gave us this declaration. I'm including it here. I suggest you say it aloud with FULL voice.

New Creation Declaration Blessing: This is who the Father says I am.

I am a new creation in Christ; the old has passed away, all things have become new. I am in Jesus; Jesus is in me. Greater is He who is in me than he who is in the world. I am a child of the king; I am a co-heirs with Jesus. All Jesus bought and paid for is my inheritance. I am loved. I am forgiven. I am cleansed by the blood. I'm accepted in the beloved. I am filled with his spirit. I am united with Jesus; I have been crucified with Christ. I died with Him. I was buried with Him. I was raised with Him. I am seated with Him in heavenly places far above all rule, all power, all authority, and above every name that is named, not only in this age, but also in the one to come.

Therefore, I carry the authority of Christ. I have authority over sickness, over sin, over demons, and over the world. I am the salt of the earth. I am more than a conqueror. I am the light of the world. All things work together for my good because I love God, and I'm a called according to his purpose, which is for me to be conformed to the image and the likeness of Christ. I can do all things through Christ, because greater is he who is in me than he who is in the world. I have a destination; I am going to heaven. In the meantime, I have an assignment; I bring heaven to earth. Everywhere I go, the kingdom of God goes. God is going to do exceedingly abundantly above all I could ask or think. I am a carrier of God's glory; where I go the atmosphere changes. I am a culture shaper, an atmosphere changer, a history maker.

Questions: Self-reflection or Group Discussion.

1. Think of one thing that resonated with you. Ask Holy Spirit why it resonated so much and is there is an activation or action step for you?
2. Whose view do you have of yourself? Whose voice are you listening to? Where do you think the voices and views come from? Pray and talk to God about it. Ask Holy Spirit to show you.
3. Review the possible sources of the voices in your head.
4. Lies can easily creep in our minds and we can partner with them. Discuss the steps of: r**ecognize, reject, repent, renounce and replace.** Identify which of these you most need to work on right now? Ask Holy Spirit to reveal things to you and believe he will as you ask.
5. On a scale of one to 10, how well do you celebrate yourself? (Read Ephesians 2:10) Discuss the magnitude of this truth and repeat this: "I know who I am, I am God's masterpiece!"
6. I've shared my mantra: "Don't Compare, Don't Compete, Celebrate!" Is this easier to do when you KNOW WHO YOU ARE?
7. Think of ways to implement this mantra. For example: when viewing Facebook, Instagram, Pinterest, driving into your own neighborhood, entering groups.
8. List ways you can better celebrate others. (co-workers, spouse, neighbors, family members, children)

Make a list:

9. Are there any additional thoughts or anything else this book/ chapters that triggered or resonated with you?
10. Pray: Thank God for your blood bought identity that is secure and hidden in Christ. Remain in an attitude of gratitude for the finished work of the Cross and your right standing with God.

Identity in Action

Here are some **action points** to apply what you've read:

1. **Be ready** - Read God's word it's your identity standard.

2. **Be listening** - Listen to God's voice through His word, preaching, God's people, dreams, visions, angelic visitations, song lyrics, the slightest impressions and a still small voice.

3. **Be open** - Allow God the time, opportunity and freedom to work in your life.

4. **Be Declaring** - Prophesy over yourself about yourself.

The power of the tongue is incredible, remember, Proverbs 18:21. I have been very affected by the words I have spoken. I say, "Our words create worlds!" Therefore, I have made it a practice to declare certain things aloud. I'd like to give a shout out to a ministry that has deeply affected and blessed my life, Igniting Hope Ministries with Steve and Wendy Backlund. I honor who they are and the message of hope they both carry. I would like to list some of the declarations that I say almost daily, it's just a portion of 100 declarations I found years ago on their website. They have given me permission to include these here.

Identity Fortifying Declarations:

- The Lord of Peace is peace. In every way, He always gives me his peace. 2 Thessalonians 3:16.

- I am confident of this very thing, that he who has begun a good work in me will complete it until the day of Christ Jesus. Philippians 1: 6.

- Christ bore my sins in His own body on the cross and I am healed by His stripes. 1 Peter 2:24.

- I am blessed with every spiritual blessing in the heavenly places in Christ. Ephesians 1:3.

- I am chosen in Christ before the foundation of the world that I may be holy and blameless before the father. Ephesians 1:4.

- Christ bore my sins in His own body on the cross and I am healed by His stripes. 1 Peter 2:24.

- I am blessed with every spiritual blessing in the heavenly places in Christ. Ephesians 1:3.

- I am chosen in Christ before the foundation of the world that I may be holy and blameless before the Father. Ephesians 1:4.

- The Father has accepted me in the beloved. Ephesians 1:6.

- I have redemption through Jesus Christ blood and the forgiveness of sins. Ephesians 1:7, Colossians 1:14.

- I have obtained an inheritance in Christ. Ephesians 1:11.

- I am sealed with the Holy Spirit who is the guarantee of my inheritance. Ephesians 1:13–14.

- God raised me up in the heavenly places to sit with Him in Jesus Christ. Ephesians 2:6.
- I am saved by grace through faith, I am not saved by my own works. Ephesians 2:8–9.

- I am God's masterpiece. He created me anew in Christ Jesus, so I can do the good things He planned for me long ago. Ephesians 2:10. NLT.

- I have been brought to the Father by the blood of Christ. Ephesians 2:13.

- I have access by one Spirit to the Father through Jesus Christ. Ephesians 2:18.

- Christ dwells in my heart by faith, I am rooted and grounded in love. Ephesians 3:17.

- God does exceedingly abundantly above all I could ask or think according to His power that works in me. Ephesians 3:20.

- God gives me the victory through Jesus Christ my Lord. 1 Corinthians 15:57.

- I thank God! He always leads me triumphantly by the Messiah and through me spreads everywhere the fragrance of knowing Him. 2 Corinthians 2:14. ISV

- I have the mind of Christ. 1 Corinthians 2:16.

- I am in Christ Jesus and therefore I am a new creation. Old things have passed away and all things have become new. 2 Corinthians 5:17.

- If I sin, I have an advocate with the Father, Jesus Christ, the righteous. 1 John 2:1 ESV.

- All of God's promises are yes and amen for me because I am in Christ. 2 Corinthians 1:20.

- I am qualified in Christ to be a partaker of the inheritance of the saints. Colossians 1:12.

- God my Father has delivered me from the power of darkness and transferred me into the kingdom of His beloved Son. Colossians 1:13.

Hallelujah!!!

Rachel Inouye is the author of Lily Pads - Stories of God on Display, He Speaks - Hearing the Voice of God Through Journaling, and its companion journal, I'm Listening.

She is the host of "the real deal" podcast, "Helping people celebrate their significance and the genius of God in them!"

Rachel is a child of The Most High God. She's a wife, mama, grandma, mentor, speaker, storyteller, worshiper and podcaster. Rachel enjoys all things people, walks, dark chocolate, movie-going, thrifting, warm weather and coffee shops. She relishes a belly laugh, healthy food and worship music. She ushers people into hope and spreads encouragement. She desires to be spotted holding hands with her husband, Michael and seen hanging out with her amazing kids and grandson.

Connect with Rachel

rachelinouye.org

Podcast: "the real deal"

Books:
Lily Pads - Stories of God on Display
He Speaks - Hearing the Voice of God Through Journaling
I'm Listening - Companion Journal to He Speaks
Available at rachelinouye.org and Amazon

YouTube: rachelinouye.org

Blog: Rachelinouye.wordpress.com

Social Media:
FaceBook: Rachel Inouye
Instagram: Rachel Inouye
Twitter: 4thgirlrach

Made in USA - Kendallville, IN
75549_9798846020887
08.24.2022 1636